MW00463827

# Periphery

# Periphery

*Israel's Search for Middle East Allies*

Yossi Alpher

ROWMAN & LITTLEFIELD
Lanham • Boulder • New York • London

Published by Rowman & Littlefield
A wholly owned subsidiary of The Rowman & Littlefield Publishing Group, Inc.
4501 Forbes Boulevard, Suite 200, Lanham, Maryland 20706
www.rowman.com

Unit A, Whitacre Mews, 26–34 Stannary Street, London SE11 4AB, United Kingdom

British Library Cataloguing in Publication Information Available

**Library of Congress Cataloging-in-Publication Data**

Alpher, Yossi.
Periphery : Israel's search for Middle East allies / Yossi Alpher.
pages cm
Includes bibliographical references and index.
ISBN 978-1-4422-3101-6 (cloth : alk. paper)—ISBN 978-1-4422-3102-3 (electronic)
1. Israel—Foreign relations. 2. Israel—Foreign relations—Middle East. 3. Middle East—Foreign relations—Israel. 4. National security—Israel. I. Title.
DS119.6.A67 2015
327.5694056—dc23
2014027169

Printed in the United States of America

**(for whom it may concern)**

What justifies most of all
the loneliness, the great despair,
the peculiar submission to the burden
of the great loneliness of the great despair,
is the simple cutting fact
we have nowhere else to go.

—David Avidan, from "Power of Attorney," 1957 (translated from the Hebrew by
Tsipi Keller)

For Rogel, Daniella, and Yariv

# Contents

## III: Conclusion

# Preface

In 1965, as a warrant officer in the Israel Defense Forces (IDF) fresh out of basic training, I was posted to General Staff Headquarters in Tel Aviv's Kirya. My assignment, under the chief education officer, was to teach English. I had no idea how to teach English, and no interest. I was furious. This was not why I had immigrated to Israel a year earlier with a bachelor of arts in oriental studies and hastened to join the army. I wanted to be a fully trained officer and serve in Intelligence. I wanted action, anything but teaching English.

One spring day, I was told to report to Lieutenant Colonel Tsuri Sagui for a special assignment. Sagui, a gruff, dark, mustachioed, red-bereted paratrooper from a moshav farming background, sat me down on one of the lawns in the Kirya base together with three other officers, all from the paratroops, and presented me with an IDF manual of basic tactics: ambushes, explosives, and the like. "We four are going to Kurdistan to help the Kurds fight the Iraqi army," Tsuri explained. "You're going to translate this manual for us into the basic English terms we'll need and teach us to use them. We can't take a Hebrew manual to Kurdistan, because officially only their leader Mulla Mustafa Barzani and his aides will know we're Israeli. In Kurdistan, someone will translate our English into Kurdish."

"I'm not sure I have security clearance for this," I volunteered naïvely.

"No time for niceties," Tsuri replied. "Let's get to work."

The Kurds, I pondered. So we have friends in the Middle East. It's not all Arab enemies.

That was my introduction to the "periphery doctrine," under which Israel sought links and alliances with non-Arab and non-Muslim countries and minorities in the Middle East, as well as with Arab states geographically distant from the Arab–Israel conflict. I would go on to a career as an IDF Intelligence officer and Mossad official, during which I would deal with "periphery" issues in depth. Frequently, these dealings were as improvised as that meeting with Tsuri Sagui, who led Israel's first military training delegation into an Arab country to work with a non-Arab minority. Indeed, they were as improvised as the army's attempt to get me to teach English.

From the Mossad in 1981 I moved to Tel Aviv University's Jaffee Center for Strategic Studies. There I "graduated" from intelligence, which looks at the other but not at ourselves, to strategy, which integrates our own profile into a broader picture. It was at the Jaffee Center that I began to look retrospectively at the periphery doctrine as a grand strategy. During those same years, while following from afar the eight year–long Iran–Iraq War, which pitted a periphery country against a "core" Arab country, I gained additional perspective regarding the doctrine.

I came to understand that not many in Israel possessed both the personal operational experience and the strategic outlook that would be necessary to write about this grand strategy. Indeed, many Middle East and security experts, both in Israel and abroad, have little or no knowledge or awareness of the periphery doctrine, not the least because it has never been properly documented and studied by the Israeli establishment. Writing about it, I realized, could be important for both Israelis and non-Israelis to understand Israel as a Middle East entity: its isolation and need to find regional friends, and the US and Jewish "angles" to Israel's identity.

Thus, some thirty years ago I began collecting material, looking toward the day when I would enjoy the leisure to write about the periphery doctrine.

I never found the leisure, yet in the past five years, I felt obliged to make the time. Two developments combined to prompt me to urgently address the task. One was sad: in 2009, when I learned of the terminal illness of a friend and former colleague, David Kimche, I realized that time was running out on the opportunity to interview many of those who had been intimately involved in periphery issues as far back as the 1950s. Dave was my first interviewee and was followed by around fifty others: former heads of Mossad, academics, journalists, government officials, Arab intellectuals, Americans who once interacted with the doctrine at work, and Greeks and Cypriots from the "new periphery."

Back in 2009 and 2010, I assumed I would be writing a kind of strategic history—a book drawing lessons from a grand strategy of the past. Then along came a dramatic boost in the rise of political Islam in Israel's neighborhood: Iran, Hezbollah, and Hamas were joined by Turkey, under Erdogan, and Egypt, under the Muslim Brotherhood. It seemed that Israel was in danger of being enveloped by a new ring of hostility, whose core embodied much of the old, friendly periphery, and that it had to at least consider the need for a new periphery to leapfrog over that ring. Suddenly, the lessons of the old, or classic, periphery of the 1950s, 1960s, and 1970s took on an entirely new relevance for Israel's present and future interaction with the region. While, at the time of writing, relations with Turkey and especially Egypt had improved, the notion of combating militant Islam with a new set of regional relationships is now very much a dimension of Israeli strategic thinking that justifies writing about the periphery doctrine.

# Acknowledgments

I am indebted to NOREF, the Norwegian Peacebuilding Resource Center, and its director, Mariano Aguirre, and to Rockefeller Brothers Fund (working through the Institute of International Education) and its president, Stephen Heintz, for their financial as well as intellectual support for the research and writing that went into this book. A monograph of mine published by NOREF in mid-2013, "Israel: Alternative Regional Options in a Changing Middle East," proved an extremely helpful research and writing experience in formulating this book.

At a more general and even historical level, my thanks to three mentors who taught me much of what I profess to know and understand about strategic thinking and analysis in a Middle East context, all of whom are mentioned in this book: Alouph Hareven, the late Yitzhak Oron, and the late Aharon Yariv.

My gratitude to all those who agreed to be interviewed and quoted (they are listed separately) and thereby shared their wisdom, experience, and insights with me. In addition, Major General (ret.) Shlomo Gazit and professors Moshe Maoz and Asher Susser read a draft manuscript and offered extremely valuable comments that challenged some of my most basic assumptions. Yona Kolman produced the maps with his usual professionalism. Nevertheless, I alone remain responsible for any mistakes embodied in the book.

The opening lines (English translation) from David Avidan's poem "Power of Attorney" are quoted with permission from Tsipi Keller (the translator) and reprinted by permission from SUNY Press, publisher of *Poets on the Edge: An Anthology of Contemporary Hebrew Poetry* (2008).

The Israel Embassy in Athens and particularly Ambassador Aryeh Mekel were extremely helpful in facilitating my research efforts there. A number of librarians and intellectual resource managers in Israel went out of their way to assist me in locating source material. My thanks to Hana Pinshow and Ofer Schiff of the Ben Gurion Archives at Sde Boker; Cecilia Harel, collection development specialist at the University of Haifa Library; Yoel Kozak of the INSS Information Center in Tel Aviv; the staff of the Dayan Center library at Tel Aviv University; and the staff of the Meir Amit Intelligence and Terrorism Information Center at the Israeli Intelligence and Heritage Commemoration Center in Ramat HaSharon.

A special thanks to my literary agent, Dorothy Harman, for so successfully navigating the ins and outs of finding a publisher.

Above and beyond all else, thanks to my wife and partner, Irene Tamar Alpher, for her unflagging support and encouragement throughout this very long project.

# Introduction

This book describes the evolution and implementation of an Israeli grand strategy, the periphery doctrine. It seeks to assess the doctrine's successes and failures and their ramifications for Israel's overall security and well-being. It concludes by considering the justification for a possible "new periphery" and the meaning of the periphery quest for Israel's identity and self-image.

Conceived by Prime Minister David Ben Gurion and his close aides in 1957–1958, the periphery doctrine (*torat haperipheria*) was apparently never embodied in an official staff paper or directive, and the precise extent or content of the periphery never defined. The doctrine's implementers, mainly in the Mossad, Israel's civilian external intelligence arm, seemingly fleshed it out on the wing in the spirit of improvisation, which has frequently character-ized Israel's search for security solutions. Even the term "periphery" was totally Israelo-centric: we, Israel, situated ostensibly in the center of the Arab Middle East (that is where we place ourselves on our maps), were surrounded by a ring of hostile Arab countries led by Egypt's president Gamal Abdel Nasser and nurtured by his aggressive Arab nationalist ideology and frequent threats to "throw the Jews into the sea." We reached beyond that ring in search of friends and allies to what was, for us, the periphery of the region.

At the conceptual level, not every Israeli involved back then in links with Turkey, the Lebanese Maronites, or the southern Sudanese pondered the significance of implementing what can be defined only as a grand strategy. Among those of us who did, not everyone agreed on what exactly the periph-ery comprised. As I learned years later in interviewing heads of Mossad for this study, even they did not necessarily think in strategic terms in their day-to-day administration of these links. In many ways, it is only in retrospect that Israel's ties with the Kurds and the Iranians, the Yemeni royalists, and

Morocco emerge as a coherent strategic doctrine—one that frequently involved a US connection as well as a Jewish dimension of immigration to Israel from countries such as Iraq, Lebanon, Morocco, and Ethiopia.

## TERMINOLOGY

In exploring the periphery doctrine, I formulated two working definitions that find expression in this book. One defines "periphery" and the other, "grand strategy" in the periphery doctrine context.

The classic periphery comprised three categories or spheres of partners: those non-Arab and non-Muslim countries that bordered on the Arab conflict states—the core—of the pre-1977 era; non-Arab and non-Muslim peoples who lived within the conflict states; and Arab states on the geographic extremes of the Middle East that felt threatened by militant Arab nationalism or had domestic or regional reasons for seeking ties with Israel. At the state level the periphery was ethnic, embodying Iran and Turkey; religious, for example, Christian Ethiopia; and geographic, including Morocco, Oman, Yemen, and Sudan. At the nonstate level of regional minorities, the periphery was ethnic and religious: Kurds, southern Sudanese, and Maronites. Not surprisingly, in view of the reference to "core" and "rings," the terms "spheres," "circles," and "doctrine of spheres" were also referred to as synonyms for "periphery doctrine."

The basis for this definition of periphery is strategic—these were the regional actors with whom Israel sought to counter Arab hostility—as well as to a lesser extent bureaucratic: this is the way the Mossad tended to "organize" contacts with them in its day-to-day workings. Most but not all of the former Mossad heads and senior officials, scholars, and others whom I interviewed agreed that this was a reasonable working definition. Some argued that Arab states, such as Morocco and Oman, could not be included in the periphery since despite their physical and political distance, they were by definition part of the Arab core. Others went so far as to assign Middle East minorities, such as the Kurds, to a different category, contending that minorities could not be lumped with periphery states such as Iran and Ethiopia.

My problem with these alternative approaches is that they seemingly ignore the fluid nature of regional relations. When the periphery doctrine was launched, Sudan, a predominantly Arab state, was lumped with Ethiopia in the "southern triangle," which was considered one of the original building blocks of the periphery doctrine. The operation in Kurdistan could not be separated from Trident, the alliance with the Iranians and Turks. The eventual emergence of Kurdistan in Iraq and South Sudan as quasi-independent or independent political entities seemingly justifies their earlier treatment as part of the political periphery. Then too, Arab observers of Israel's periphery strategy tend to understand and recognize it according to this more inclusive version (see chapter 14).

Defining what constitutes a possible new periphery is equally problematic. First it is necessary to define the new, Islamist core: Iran, Sudan, Hamas in Gaza, Hezbollah in southern Lebanon, and if it emerges from its civil war under Islamist rule, possibly Syria. But Turkey and Egypt are included only insofar as they are under the sway of hostile Islamists, and by 2014 this was not their constant state. Compared to the original Arab nationalist core, the recent Islamist core is geographically and ethnically far more expansive, dictating a more far-flung periphery, which includes European states that share land and sea borders with Turkey (Cyprus, Greece, and Bulgaria); states bordering on Iran; Ethiopia, South Sudan, and Kenya; and possibly Eritrea to the south of Egypt and of Sudan, near the critical Bab al-Mandeb Straits and Red Sea shipping routes. At the time of writing, this new periphery did not comprise any minorities—reflecting the negative legacy of the 1982–1983 fiasco with the Maronites—though events in and around Syria could at some point in the future affect that calculation as well.

Some Israeli strategic thinkers I have consulted with would expand the new periphery to include Romania and India. Others would list the Central Asian "stans" of the former Soviet Union. Some insist on looking farther west into Europe, toward Albania and even Italy, in search of a Mediterranean identity. My inclination—given the newness, novelty, and tenuous nature of the new periphery concept; the fluid nature of the new Islamist core; and the substantive differences that distinguish both the new core and the new periphery from the old, classic core and periphery—is to opt for a minimalist definition. Indeed, as events unfold in key countries such as Turkey and Egypt, it is perforce necessary to question the entire new periphery concept.

Thus when it comes to understanding the periphery concept at work, all these alternative visions, definitions, and doubts are valid. Hopefully, these concepts will contribute to the debate over the issues that this book seeks to raise. In researching and writing it, I certainly had no intention to challenge the collective wisdom of colleagues from academia and the security and intelligence communities. After all, the periphery doctrine was never enshrined in an official codex, and its modalities are wide open to constructive interpretation.

In contrast, I would argue that the use of the term "grand strategy" to define not only the periphery doctrine but also the "sister" doctrines that emerged earlier or simultaneously under Ben Gurion's leadership—linking up with a great power or superpower, rapid mass Jewish immigration, and developing a nuclear deterrent—is less subject to challenge. All four doctrines sought to ensure Israel's long-term security at the highest existential level by employing an integrated assortment of diplomatic and military strategies that covered a broad geographic expanse over an extended time span. None of the many veterans of the classic periphery doctrine that I queried contested this definition or the broad set of principles it embodies. Whether the term "grand strategy" applies to the new periphery is perhaps more open to discussion in view of the fluid and even revolutionary nature of events in core countries such as Egypt, coupled with the relatively weak "lineup" of the new periphery states. Time will tell.

Two concluding remarks are in order concerning methodology. On the one hand, moving from grand strategy to tactics, where appropriate I have introduced anecdotes based on personal experience of the periphery at the operational, analytic, and research levels. The idea is to lighten and add color to an otherwise straightforward, descriptive text. Hopefully, in this way I can also share with the reader a taste of the intelligence work that went into building and maintaining the periphery doctrine.

On the other hand, each individual periphery operation is described relatively briefly, the idea being to focus on only those aspects that are relevant to the broader strategic fabric of the narrative. Readers who wish to pursue the study of a specific case or operation will find ample references in the endnotes—although, notably, many of them refer to Hebrew texts.

## SOURCES

The book draws on three categories of sources. One is my own direct experience for nearly thirty years in the intelligence and strategic fields. Where no other source is mentioned regarding Mossad operations and activity, I am the source. Additional personal knowledge has been culled from travels and broad regional contacts in later years, including recent visits to Cyprus and Greece undertaken specifically with the objective of understanding the thinking behind the concept of a new periphery.

A second set of sources is published material, including media coverage of periphery issues over the years and histories and memoirs, among them books written specifically about unique periphery operations, for example in Kurdistan.

Finally, but by no means least, are the many interviews I conducted: with former heads of Mossad, academics, journalists, government officials, Arab intellectuals, Americans who once interacted with the periphery doctrine, and Greeks and Cypriots from the new periphery. In a few cases, interviewees still in government service or from Arab countries remain anonymous, at their request. Here it also bears mention that a conscious decision was made to limit new periphery travel and interviews to the two Hellenic Mediterranean countries. There, unlike in other countries that are considered central to a possible new periphery, I could have unfettered access to willing and knowledgeable sources who were not constrained by regime or governmental intimidation in expressing their views freely.

Obviously, this means that coverage of additional new periphery countries draws strictly on Israeli sources and the media—a drawback that should be borne in mind by the reader. That information gathering in and about autocratic countries can be a critical lacuna with regard to decision making about them is one of the conclusions pointed to in the final chapter of this book.

Finally, I approached the topic of the periphery doctrine as a former intelligence professional with experience in strategic analysis. I made a conscious decision to prefer interviews with surviving periphery veterans, coupled with my own recollections, to a comprehensive search of the academic literature and archives that deal with Israeli strategy and Israel's Middle East relations. This reflects my perception that both sources are seriously deficient in their discussion of the periphery doctrine as a grand strategy. Israel's "Arabists," for perhaps understandable reasons, have preferred to deal mainly with Israel–Arab affairs. As renowned a strategic thinker as Yehoshafat Harkabi never even mentions the periphery doctrine in a series of distinguished works.

Obviously, this book does not even begin to exhaust the quest for a better understanding of Israeli periphery thinking, but hopefully it makes a contribution that will be judged unique.

## STRUCTURE AND CONTENT

Three of the four maps presented in this book are designed to offer a graphic presentation of the original periphery doctrine, with the exception of Morocco, which proved impossible to work in both conceptually and in terms of the geography of map making. A fourth map, "A new periphery?" seeks to convey both the content of Israel's projected new "axes of containment" and the element of doubt that pervades our analysis of this emerging concept.

The first part of this book presents the periphery doctrine at work. It opens in chapter 1 with a discussion of the doctrine's origins and then proceeds to present each major operation or theater of operations.

Trident, the Israeli–Iranian–Turkish alliance, is discussed in chapter 2 in terms of its important and early contribution to Israel's deterrent profile but also with reference to the Iranians' and Turks' ambiguous and highly compartmentalized attitude toward Israel. Trident ended with the fall of the shah in 1979.

Next, in chapter 3, Israel's periphery relationship with Morocco focuses on that country's unique Jewish and Amazigh (Berber) heritage, which played a central role in creating and sustaining ties.

Chapter 4, on the southern periphery, brings together a broad selection of periphery ties, from Ethiopia beginning in the mid-1950s, through clandestine Israeli military aid to the Yemeni royalists in the mid-1960s, to the southern Sudanese operation of the late 1960s and early 1970s. All in all, and seen in historical perspective, Israel's southern periphery operations appear to have registered relatively unambiguous successes in terms of Israel's security requirements.

This stands out in sharp contrast with Israel's involvement with Levant minorities, discussed in chapter 5, which began decades before Israeli independence in 1948 but which ended—at least pending possible developments in the Syrian civil war—with the First Lebanon War of 1982–1983. The prestate search for ties with Levant Christians and Druze provides interesting commentary on the early phases of Israel's quest for a regional identity.

Finally, in chapter 6, Israel's aid to the Kurds of northern Iraq is discussed. Like the southern Sudanese operation, the Kurdish relationship reflects a rather special humanitarian and emotional aspect of Israeli support for fellow Middle East minorities suffering from Arab oppression. This merits attention because it portrays what is for some a surprisingly noble and noncynical aspect of the Israeli national personality.

In chapters 7 and 8, respectively, the narrative then briefly discusses two additional highly relevant strategic aspects of the periphery doctrine in its early days. The Jewish dimension focuses on *aliyah*, or immigration, to Israel from the periphery—Morocco and Ethiopia, as well as Kurdish help to Jews escaping Iraq. The US dimension centers on Israel's success in marketing its periphery ties to Washington and obtaining CIA financial support but also highlights the limitations of Washington's interest.

By the late 1970s and early 1980s, the periphery doctrine appeared to have run its course. The periphery itself had seemingly collapsed. The Kurds were cut off from Israeli access in 1975. The shah of Iran and Emperor Haile Selassie of Ethiopia fell from power in the late 1970s, to be replaced with hostile or unfriendly rulers. In 1982, Israel's alliance with the Lebanese Maronites generated a tragic fiasco. Thus ended a concerted attempt to give Israel a Middle East regional identity based on affiliation with the non-Arabs and non-Muslims of the region. Chapter 9 discusses these developments and concludes part I.

Part II looks at ramifications of the periphery doctrine and the periphery period. It opens with chapter 10, which assesses "periphery nostalgia," a phenomenon that still generates problematic Israeli attitudes toward Islamist Turkey and particularly Iran, as illustrated by the Iran–Contra affair. Periphery nostalgia is very much a reflection of the different and at times even desperate way Israelis have treated their relationship with the non-Arab and non-Muslim actors of the Middle East—in contrast with the way the latter viewed Israel.

Chapter 11 follows with a presentation of the views, dating back to the 1950s, of Israeli skeptics who criticized the periphery doctrine, whether because of a perceived cost–benefit deficit or the alleged negative effect of the pursuit of periphery ties on efforts to make inroads to peace with the Arab core. The 1973 Yom Kippur War and the demise of the Kurdish operation were key catalysts of skepticism. While with historical hindsight these views appear to this author less than viable, they are important to keep in mind if Israel is to avoid making such mistakes with a possible new periphery and a very different core.

Between 1973 and 1983 the periphery doctrine and Israel's regional fortunes underwent radical change. The demise of the periphery and the setbacks of Trident, the Kurdish relationship, and the Maronite adventure were seemingly more than balanced by the advent of peace with Israel's Arab neighbors, beginning in 1977 with Egypt at the Sunni Arab core—a peace facilitated, not accidentally, by Iran and particularly Morocco, two periphery friends. The Palestinian issue became, for better or worse, the focus of Israel's relations with the region. After the Oslo breakthrough of 1993, Israel briefly sought to become a conventional regional "player," open to pragmatic relations with one and all, Arabs and non-Arabs. With international backing, it boosted grandiose plans for regional multilateral cooperation. That aspiration, too, was dashed in short order.

This "between peripheries" narrative is discussed in chapter 12. It is followed in chapter 13 by a presentation of new periphery thinking and its conceptual underpinnings, advantages, and drawbacks against the backdrop of the "Arab spring" and the rise of political Islam in many of the Arab and Muslim countries surrounding Israel. We then pause in chapter 14 for a presentation of Arab reaction to the periphery concept, an issue of particular relevance for the new periphery and especially for the case of Egypt, against the backdrop of the new southern periphery and a possible crisis over Nile waters.

In this regard, as the concluding chapter emphasizes, Israel could conceivably be seen by its neighbors, albeit unfairly, as a factor in the Nile crisis or, alternatively, as a regional actor seeking to develop a unique role in bridging core–periphery dilemmas. This final chapter, which focuses on Israel's search for a regional identity, reassesses the successes and failures of the original periphery, the rationale of a new periphery to the extent that it exists, and the overall ramifications of this grand strategy for Israel's role and status in the Middle East region.

Drawing on the discussion of the original periphery and the Arab response, the book's conclusions emphasize the need to avoid zero-sum thinking in developing a new periphery. The new Islamist core emerging fitfully in the Middle East still offers compelling opportunities for Israel to pursue engagement.

Finally, in chapter 15, our conclusions address the very central dilemma of Israel–Arab peace. Did the original periphery doctrine help or hinder peace? Will some sort of emerging new axes of containment help or hinder? That depends to a large extent on how this new concept is formulated and managed, and how the issue of peace and coexistence with Israel's immediate Arab neighbors, and particularly the Palestinians, is dealt with at the strategic level by the country's leadership.

All told, the insights this book seeks to transmit may be summarized as follows:

1. The classic periphery doctrine was a viable grand strategy. A cost–benefit analysis demonstrates that it succeeded to a far greater extent than it failed.
2. Israel's periphery approach to regional minorities was noble.
3. In general, the classic periphery doctrine was not understood by the Israeli strategic leadership as a zero-sum game vis-à-vis opportunities for peace but rather as a means of leveraging peace with Israel's Arab neighbors, which is far more important and has proven more long lasting than have periphery alliances.
4. The periphery doctrine worked in tandem with additional grand strategies: close ties to a great power, beginning with France and the United Kingdom and culminating in the United States, and the massive in-gathering of the exiles.
5. Today, as a regional power with global strategic and economic reach, Israel should address the countries of the Middle East as a mosaic of Arabs and non-Arabs, Islamists and non-Islamists, core and periphery. Links to all are possible, and conceivably Israel can even fill a mediating role among them.
6. Based on lessons drawn from the classic periphery, relations with a new periphery should be founded on interests and not sentiment. The bigger Israel's investment in new periphery ties, the more it must invest in intelligence to prevent strategic surprises like the fall of the shah in 1979.
7. The economic dimension is far more prominent in the new periphery than in the old.
8. Ben Gurion's original grand strategies were ambitious yet were realized. This is not the case with Israel's current strategic performance.

*I*

# The Periphery Doctrine at Work

# Chapter One

# Evolution of a Grand Strategy

The periphery doctrine of Israel's early decades was a grand strategy, meaning an endeavor to recruit and channel the country's resources toward the attainment of a major political–security goal: in this case, countering Arab hostility through relations with alternative regional powers and potential allies over a period of years.

The periphery doctrine emerged in the mid-1950s in the thinking of David Ben Gurion and his close advisers—particularly Reuven Shiloah, who founded the Mossad, and Iser Harel, who headed both the Mossad and the Shin Bet (Israel's domestic intelligence and counterespionage service) from the early 1950s.[1] It was a consequence, or lesson, derived from Israel's 1948–1949 War of Independence and the 1956 Sinai campaign: Israel had to broaden its regional reach, go beyond the circle of hostile Arab states surrounding it to the periphery of the region (periphery, from an Israelo-centric point of view), and enter into close security relations with states and minorities there that shared Israel's threat assessment regarding the Arabs. As Mossad head Meir Amit would explain to a skeptical Prime Minister Levi Eshkol in 1966, "[W]e have an interest in principle in getting in touch with every minority in the Middle East. We have an interest in acting against the thesis that we are a foreign body in the region, and in proving that the Middle East is not made of a single fabric."[2]

The periphery doctrine also reflected the assessment of Ben Gurion and Shiloah that key events in the Middle East—revolution in Iraq and unrest in Jordan and Lebanon in 1958 and growing Soviet penetration—warranted a concerted attempt by Israel to build alliances with Turkey and Iran and to sell these alliances to the United States and NATO as a means of aggrandizing Israel's importance to the Western alliance, thereby enhancing its security.

3

At the heart of this thinking was the acute realization, born of two wars and more to come, that Israel was surrounded by enemies that continued to seek its destruction despite their defeat on the battlefield. Further, as Israelis learned after 2,000 years of Diaspora to think in sovereign terms anchored in the country's geostrategic reality, they recalled that throughout their earlier sovereign history, in biblical times, they had always sought to make alliances with strong powers in the extended neighborhood to ensure survival. Not accidentally, many of the periphery states and peoples—Iran, Ethiopia, the Kurds, the Maronites—had roots in the Middle East that by far predated the Arabs, thereby reaffirming for the new state of Israel its own national narrative of ancient historic and religious roots in the Middle East.

The ancient Hebrews had learned to develop, in the words of former Mossad head Ephraim Halevy, "a regional and great power strategy."[3] During the days of the prophets, they turned toward either Babylon or Egypt. In more modern times, World War I, a small vanguard of strategic innovators, the Nili underground, led the transition from an Ottoman to a British orientation.[4] "This is embedded in the DNA of the Jewish people: it must always rely on certain regional and international actors."[5] Modern Israel's founders also realized that a sovereign Hebrew state or states had existed in the Holy Land for but a few centuries out of over 1,000 years of pre-Diaspora Israelite presence. This was a chilling warning to the modern state's founders of just how fragile the Jewish state's long-term prospects were.

The precise origins of the term "periphery doctrine" (*torat haperipheria*) are not clear; apparently, Shiloah coined it. At some early stage it simply emerged as an accurate description of what was developing on the ground and on the map. Ben Gurion and his advisers were convinced that Israel's Arab neighbors, led by Egyptian President Gamal Abdel Nasser, were not candidates for peace treaties with Israel or even for serious peaceful coexistence. On the contrary, having failed to destroy the nascent Jewish state when it was created in 1948, they were trying to choke it with an economic boycott and with guerilla or fedayeen attacks across its borders, and were arming for additional rounds of warfare.

Notably, a school of thought led by Moshe Sharett, who served as foreign minister and briefly as prime minister during the 1950s, argued that a greater effort should be made by Israel to develop the 1949 armistice agreements with its neighbors into peace agreements. This is one primary source of criticism of the periphery doctrine: that it came at the expense of an enhanced effort to reach accommodation with the Arab core. It will be revisited in chapter 11, which deals with Israeli skeptics.

In his diary entries for mid-1958, when the Trident alliance with Iran and Turkey—the centerpiece of the periphery strategy—was taking shape, Ben Gurion refers to additional factors warranting Israeli security concern: the Syrian–Egyptian union, a radical coup d'etat in Iraq, and emergency deployments of US troops to Lebanon and British troops to Jordan.[6] Moreover, as the aftermath of the 1956 Sinai campaign demonstrated—when Ben Gurion yielded to a US–Soviet ultimatum to withdraw from the captured Sinai Peninsula and Gaza Strip—Israel's retaliatory options against Arab aggression were constrained by international circumstance.[7]

The periphery doctrine was in fact one of four interrelated grand strategies that emerged in Israeli security circles under Ben Gurion in the country's first decade and that guided Israel's security behavior for years to come—in some cases, to this day.

As it developed, the periphery strategy dovetailed nicely with two of them: the ingathering of the exiles and the need for a great power ally.

The periphery strategy interacted with the strategy of great power alliance in two principal ways. On the one hand, as Israel developed alliance-type relationships with Iran, Turkey, and Ethiopia and a military assistance presence among the Kurds of northern Iraq, it successfully marketed these relationships to the American security community, which saw in them promising assets against Soviet inroads into the Arab Middle East and a counterbalance to pro-Soviet regimes in Egypt, Syria, and Iraq. In some instances, this produced useful intelligence exchanges; in others, Washington was even induced to provide budgetary assistance to Israel's military effort. In other words, the doctrine put Israel "on the map" of the Greater Middle East, or in the words of veteran senior intelligence analyst Yitzhak Oron, "we were counted"[8]—a source of no little satisfaction to a beleaguered, isolated country.

In the summer of 1958, Ben Gurion wrote to the leaders of the United States and France that "our goal is to create a group of countries, not necessarily a formal and public alliance, that . . . will be able to stand fast against Soviet expansion via Nasser. . . . This group will comprise two non-Arab Muslim states (Persia and Turkey), a Christian country (Ethiopia) and Israel."[9] He then noted US Secretary of State John Foster Dulles's readiness to "indicate to Turkey and Iran our feeling of satisfaction that there are developing ties" between them and Israel.[10]

But the United States balked at Israel's attempt, spearheaded by Shiloah and apparently by IDF Chief of Staff Moshe Dayan,[11] to leverage these relationships into NATO membership. Nor could all periphery relationships be shopped to the United States and receive Washington's blessings. In the late 1970s, when Israel sought to make inroads with the Mengistu regime in Ethiopia, Prime Minister Menachem Begin failed to sell the Carter administration on the wisdom of the move, apparently due to considerations relating to Mengistu's problematic human rights record. Earlier, Israel's military intervention in Yemen in 1964–1967, on the side of the royalists and in concert with an unofficial, hence deniable, British effort, collided with

Washington's initial approval of the Egyptian-backed republican takeover there.

Indeed, prior to and in parallel with the early development of the Israeli–US relationship, Israel maintained aspects of a great power association with both the French and the British. The three actors' collusion in launching the October 1956 Sinai/Suez campaign is the best-known instance, and for more than a decade Paris was the IDF's primary arms supplier. Early connections with Ethiopia were coordinated with France, [12] which welcomed intelligence and military ties with Israel in view of support by Egypt's Nasser regime for the anti-French Algerian insurrection. But it was the British, with whom the relationship really began during WWI and who also supplied weapons to Israel through the 1960s, who were key—usually acting informally or "unofficially"—to the development of the Israeli–Sudanese relationship in 1954–1958, the Omani relationship after 1975, and the Yemeni intervention.

Interaction between the periphery doctrine and the ingathering of the exiles was an almost knee-jerk by-product wherever circumstances seemed favorable. Obviously, a close intelligence relationship with Iran and Turkey helped ensure that the Jewish populations of these countries could immigrate to Israel unfettered. Less obvious is the chain of cause and effect whereby collaboration with Iran provided Israel with access to the Iraqi Kurds, who subsequently helped smuggle Jews from the Arab cities of Iraq to Kurdistan in the north, from where they proceeded to Iran and then to Israel. The ingathering of the Ethiopian Jewish community proved even more difficult to effect, despite the Israeli–Ethiopian relationship. Yet without that link and ties in Sudan it would have been near impossible to organize. Finally, the Israeli–Moroccan relationship went virtually hand in hand with the huge Moroccan Jewish migration to Israel of the 1950s and 1960s.

The periphery doctrine interacted with chances for peace with Israel's Arab neighbors. Detractors argue that it interfered with peace insofar as it distracted Israeli policy makers from openings and opportunities to talk to the Arabs and to the extent it became known to the Arabs, signaled them that Israel was working with their rivals and enemies against Arab interests. But there is little evidence to support this claim in Arab discourse or in the opinions expressed by Arab intellectuals interviewed on this topic.

Indeed, it can also be argued that the periphery served as a vehicle of access to the Arabs and, in some cases, a means of leveraging their respect. If an Israeli alliance with Iran and Turkey could persuade the Arabs that Israel's powerful friends rendered it invincible, perhaps they would come around to make peace with it. If Israel's presence in Ethiopia and South Sudan generated (totally unfounded) Egyptian fears regarding Nile water supply, perhaps Egypt would seek ways to coexist with Israel. Certainly, some of the roots of the peace breakthrough with Egypt in 1977 were in the periphery: the shah of Iran passed messages between Israel and Egyptian President Anwar Sadat,[13] and Morocco served as a venue for high-level Israeli–Egyptian contacts that paved the way for peace. Israeli leaders such as Menachem Begin and Yitzhak Rabin consulted with the shah and the king of Morocco regarding peace not only with Egypt but also with Syria.[14]

The origins of the periphery doctrine also must be examined in terms of the categories of ethnic and political entities Israel linked up with. In all cases, because the relationships focused to a large extent on intelligence and clandestine activity, the Israeli institution that implemented the doctrine was the Mossad, even when as in the case of Turkey, Iran, and Ethiopia, diplomatic relations were maintained by the Israeli foreign ministry at one level or another and even when periphery relationships generated good business, as in the case of Iran and Oman (oil imports).

The non-Arab and non-Muslim states of the region, Iran, Turkey, and Ethiopia, provided the original concept of periphery in the mid-1950s. But Arab states that were peripheral geographically, hence distant from the Arab–Israel conflict and relatively free to address Israel secretly—Morocco and Oman—were quickly engaged, too. Indeed, newly independent Sudan was briefly matched with Ethiopia in what was deemed (with Israel) the "southern triangle" (Iran and Turkey completed the "northern triangle"). As we shall see, the northern triangle was the closest Israel ever came to membership in an alliance.

Finally, Israel's interest in other non-Arab and non-Muslim minorities in the region, which began in the prestate period, came to be acknowledged by most periphery policy practitioners and senior Mossad officials consulted[15] as part of the periphery doctrine: in effect, an ethnic periphery, regardless of specific geographic location. In looking at the Middle East minorities, most of which at one point or another came knocking at Israel's door seeking support (whereas periphery ties with other sovereign countries were usually commenced at Israel's initiative[16]), five criteria appear to have been central in determining whether Israel developed a significant relationship with them.[17]

First, control over territory. The Iraqi Kurds, the Syrian and Lebanese Druze, the Lebanese Maronites, and the southern Sudanese all exercised full or partial military control over territory. On the other hand the Egyptian Copts, who were never a periphery partner, did not.

Second, access. The Maronites could be reached by sea and the Kurds, via Iran and Turkey. The Syrian Druze, in Jebel Druze, some 90 kilometers distant from Upper Galilee (and after 1967, 75 kilometers from the Golan), could not be reached without fighting a territorial war with Syria. Hence a series of plans to link up with them never reached fruition. And when Iran cut off access to Iraqi Kurdistan in 1975 (Turkey never allowed it), the Israeli–Kurdish periphery relationship ended.

Third, readiness to fight a common enemy. Here too, the Kurds and Maronites stand out, though the latter ultimately tried to leave the fighting to Israel. This criterion rendered the Druze doubtful allies and eliminated the Copts.

Fourth, satisfying an Israeli strategic need. The Kurds and southern Sudanese could provide intelligence regarding an enemy Arab country (Iraq and Sudan, respectively) and could hopefully pin down Arab military units, which might otherwise be fighting Israel. The Berber mountain peoples of Morocco and Algeria, who also on occasion sought Israeli support, were too distant to qualify and in the case of Morocco, linked to a periphery friend.

Fifth, cost. The periphery doctrine was not expensive to implement. Years of clandestine activity among a minority such as the Kurds or the southern Sudanese cost little; Israeli arms supplies were taken mainly from Arab weapons captured in Israel's wars. In some cases, Mossad representatives in countries such as Iran and Ethiopia were able to facilitate Israeli arms sales and oil purchases on favorable terms. Obviously, a cheap strategy is easier to decide upon than an expensive one, for example, Israel's nuclear program.

A sixth, more nebulous and minor criterion bears mention. Some of the Israeli practitioners of the periphery doctrine regarding ethnic minorities developed humanitarian motives. Israel maintained medical missions in Iraqi Kurdistan and southern Sudan throughout its security assistance operations in these regions. It extended far-reaching agricultural and other aid in Iran and Ethiopia. This can be seen as a "hearts and minds" operation, as romanticism, as pure generosity on Israel's part, or as an effective display of "soft power."

At least one Israeli prime minister, Menachem Begin, openly identified with the Lebanese Maronites as beleaguered Christians struggling against Islam. Golda Meir is described by a former Mossad head as "viewing the link with the Kurds definitely as humanitarian, emotional, aid to an oppressed minority."[18] Even the link with Ethiopia—a periphery state rather than a minority—is described by several former senior Mossad officials as based to an extent on sentiment: the story of King Solomon and the Queen of Sheba, a shared history that is understood by Ethiopian Christians as their formative narrative.

Uzi Arad, a former national security adviser and senior Mossad official, terms this approach "the ethnic nostalgia thing. . . . [W]e started to identify with their struggles." The problem with this "monogamous" approach—"projecting on to [an ethnic minority] our state of mind"—was that it prevented Israel from cynically working both sides of an ethnic struggle, for example the Lebanese Shi'ites as well as the Maronites, and led to Israel's being exploited cynically by the Maronites.[19] Yet this approach was by no means characteristic of all the Israelis involved. And there were variations: one former head of Mossad placed Israel vis-à-vis the Kurds as "westerners who shared no identity with these minorities."[20]

In examining the successes and failures of the periphery doctrine, it emerges that no hard-and-fast criteria were ever established for judging the efficacy of any single relationship. This corresponds with the improvised nature of virtually the entire periphery operation: essentially, it was based on what worked. As David Kimche, a veteran Mossad operative and the first Israeli to visit Iraqi Kurdistan put it, "The Mossad did not think all the time in grand strategic terms. . . . There would be an important actor in the Middle East that we had no connections with, and we would ask, 'Why develop ties?' Because they don't hate us and they share our approach."[21]

True, at various times Israeli officials and strategic thinkers found reason to criticize periphery operations and even the entire doctrine. For example, at one point a senior official in the Israeli foreign ministry, Yael Vered, complained to the Mossad that its operation in Iraqi Kurdistan was getting in the way of Israeli–Turkish diplomatic ties.[22] But just as periphery operations were never based on a specific concept document handed down from generation to generation—all former Mossad heads and senior officials testified to this—so there were no institutional deliberations over what might have gone wrong with the concept.

Rather, the doctrine quietly died out in the late 1970s and early 1980s when strategic partners—the shah of Iran, the Kurds, Emperor Haile Selassie of Ethiopia—disappeared from the scene, or (the Maronites) let Israel down, or because peace with Egypt meant that the Arab core was finally less hostile and more accessible, hence making the periphery less important. To a considerable extent, the Arab hostility of the early decades would never repeat itself. True, throughout the 1980s and 1990s and the first decade of the twenty-first century a genuine normalization of Israel–Arab relations would never take place, and the Arab world would continue to view Israel as a foreign implant and Western outpost. Yet a foundation of commercial relations of one sort or another with many Arab states was laid during these years along with frosty but strategically vital peace treaties with Egypt and Jordan, and Israel had the luxury of differentiating less than before between Arab enemies and non-Arab friends in the region.

Yet the periphery doctrine began to reappear after 2010, as years of Arab state disfunction spawned a new era of Arab revolution. The rise of political Islam in Egypt and Turkey, Gaza and southern Lebanon, and Syria, coupled with the more veteran hostile Islamic regime in Iran, generated concern in Israel that it was again being surrounded by a ring of hostile states—in this case, Islamist rather than Arab nationalist.

# NOTES

1. The birth of the doctrine is related in detail in Haggai Eshed, *Reuven Shiloah: The Man Behind the Mossad*, Frank Cass, 1997; and Michael Bar-Zohar, *Ben-Gurion* (Hebrew), Zmora-Bitan, 1987.

2. Meir Amit, *Head to Head* (Hebrew), 1999, Hed Arzi, p. 165.

3. Ephraim Halevy interview, July 11, 2012.

4. Uzi Arad interview, July 17, 2012, and Halevy interview.

5. Halevy interview.

6. Ben Gurion diaries, Aug. 4, 1958, Ben Gurion archives.

7. Ami Gloska, *Haaretz Weekly*, p. 10, June 3, 2011.

8. Yitzhak Oron interview, June 16, 2010.

9. Bar-Zohar, p. 1328.

10. Ben Gurion diaries, July 25, 1958.

11. Bar-Zohar, p. 1324.

12. Bar-Zohar, p. 1322.

13. Menahem Navot interview, Dec. 26, 2010.

14. Shabtai Shavit interview, Dec. 25, 2011.

15. See also Ephraim Kahana, *Historical Dictionary of Israeli Intelligence*, Scarecrow Press, 2002, p. 229.

16. Uri Lubrani interview, July 27, 2009.

17. For an alternative classification of Middle East minorities, see Gabriel Ben Dor, Dayan Center Colloquium at Tel Aviv University, April 25, 1994, Dayan Center Library, Tel Aviv University. Ben Dor distinguishes among territorially compact minorities, such as Druze and Alawites; semicompact minorities, such as the Kurds; diffuse or scattered minorities, such as the Orthodox Christians; and semidiffuse minorities, the Egyptian Copts.

18. Nahum Admoni interview, July 27, 2011.

19. Arad interview.

20. Admoni interview.

21. David Kimche interview, July 12, 2009.

22. Aluf Hareven interview, January 3, 2012.

## Chapter Two

# The Northern Triangle

## *Iran and Turkey*

An Israeli strategic and intelligence alliance of sorts with Iran and Turkey was undoubtedly the most far-reaching and comprehensive accomplishment of the periphery doctrine. It was the flagship operation. It was called Trident, and it came into being in the course of high-level Israeli contacts with Tehran and Ankara during 1956–1958. It lasted more than twenty years, until the fall of the shah of Iran in 1979. Israel's strategic relationship with Turkey continued on and off for several decades thereafter, ending—at least for the time being—when Turkish Prime Minister Recep Tayyip Erdoğan turned against Israel in 2009–2010. Israel's extremely limited post-Trident strategic links with Iran are discussed in chapter 10, which deals with periphery nostalgia.

Trident, known in Hebrew as *kalil* (meaning complete or perfect), may have been an alliance, but it was never set to paper as an official document.[1] It did, however, function in accordance with an agreed-on routine: twice-yearly meetings of the three countries' highest intelligence officials, rotating among the three and breaking down into two discussion forums, one dealing with intelligence and the other with security or counterespionage. In between, intelligence on the Arabs and Soviets was exchanged on a near-daily basis.

The "Jewish factor" was not negligible in Trident. Both Iran and Turkey were well aware of Jewish influence in the United States and perceived a close relationship with Israel as a means of ensuring that the US Jewish lobby, urged on at strategic junctures by Israel, would press the administration regarding their needs: countering the Armenian and Greek lobbies for the Turks and ensuring a good press and positive administration and congressional attitude toward the shah despite attacks on his human rights record, particularly by Iranian students and exiles in the United States. There was a sentimental aspect as well: in broad regional, historical terms, Iran was seen by Israelis as heir to the ancient Persian king Cyrus, who allowed the exiled Jews of Babylon to return to the land of Israel in around 538 BC, and Xerxes, the king who married the Jewess Esther and saved the Jews from destruction in around 355 BC. In parallel, Turkey boasted of its excellent record in sheltering Jews, whether fleeing from the Spanish inquisition of 1492 or from the Nazis during the 1930s.

Marginal as these historical considerations might seem, they were important to Israelis and occasionally useful for Israel's partners. For example, Özdem Sanberk, the senior Turkish diplomat who negotiated the Mavi Marmara apology in 2011–2013, explained the Turkish attitude toward Trident in precisely these terms: "For Turks the friendship and solidarity with the Jewish people have always been part of the legacy of what was then called the Ottoman and nowadays the Turkish people and they are deeply rooted in our history."[2]

Sanberk may in fact not know much more about Trident than this platitude. For Israel, Trident clearly represented the vanguard of the periphery doctrine—a grand strategy. Accordingly, its foreign policy and military establishments were made aware of Trident with the objective of leveraging it to expand Israel's bilateral ties with Iran and Turkey to the maximum degree possible. This does not appear to have been the case with Iran and Turkey, where the intelligence services compartmentalized the Israeli link, often to an extreme degree.[3] One Turkish scholar estimates that no more than twenty Turks were aware of the foundation of Trident.[4] They were presumably nearly all from military intelligence.

The US dimension was also critical. From the outset, David Ben Gurion marketed Trident to the Eisenhower administration as an asset to the West against Soviet inroads into the Middle East and against Arab radicalism, particularly after Iraq withdrew from the Baghdad Pact.[5] The CIA financed construction in Israel of a two-story building intended to serve as Trident headquarters, with a "blue section" for the Iranians and a "yellow section" for the Turks on the ground floor and meeting rooms upstairs, but since the twice-yearly meetings ended up rotating among the three countries, the building was empty most of the time and was soon converted to a Mossad training facility.[6] Classified documents from the US embassy in Tehran published by the Iranian radical students who took over that building in 1979 reflect a keen US interest in the workings of Trident and in Israeli–Iranian relations in general.[7] For their part, both Iran and Turkey assessed that partnership with Israel would help ensure US backing for efforts to block Soviet subversion.[8]

## ORIGINS OF TRIDENT

Both Iran and Turkey voted against the creation of the state of Israel by the United Nations in 1947; neither supported Israel's request for UN membership in 1949. Nevertheless, both proceeded to recognize Israel on a de facto basis and to establish low-level or thinly concealed (Israel's "trade mission" in Tehran) relations. Ankara never agreed to full-fledged ambassadorial relations throughout the Trident period; Tehran never agreed until the fall of the shah in 1979 and the severance of all relations.

Neither Iran nor Turkey impeded immigration of Jews to Israel, facilitated by representatives of the Jewish Agency for Israel; in 1949–1950, Iran allowed a Mossad emissary to coordinate passage of Iraqi Jews through Tehran until they were able to leave Iraq directly. It was Iran, under Mossadeq, that first permitted the export of oil to Israel—a commercial link, using non-Israeli dummy companies, that would expand over the years into Iranian investment in the Eilat–Ashkelon pipeline linking the Red and Mediterranean seas and facilitating export of Iranian oil via Israel to Europe. In at least one instance during the early years, the payment by Israel of a bribe to a high-level official enabled the upgrading of relations.[9]

In entering into relations with Israel and then maintaining them at a low and often deniable level, Iran and Turkey, both Muslim states bordering on the Arab world, appeared to share a number of motives. Relations with the Arab countries involved both tensions and benefits, and raising and lowering the flame of ties to Israel could be useful in managing Arab links. The advantages of relations with Israel in the US context quickly became apparent. Consular issues were also prominent: Iranians and Turks held property in Israel. Five hundred Baha'is who fled during Israel's War of Independence and wished to return were Iranian subjects.[10]

There were regional geostrategic incentives, too. Israel's achievements in the 1956 Sinai campaign and the increasingly radical behavior of the Nasser regime in Egypt, the coup that brought down the monarchy in Iraq in 1958, and growing fears of Soviet incursion all came together to bring Israel, Iran, and Turkey into an intelligence relationship. Turkey's readiness to enter into secret ties with Israel and Iran reflected not only Ankara's Cold War apprehensions regarding Soviet influence in Egypt, Syria, and Iraq, but the Turks also harbored resentment over Arab support for the Greek position in the Cyprus conflict. They were involved in territorial disputes with Syria and water disputes with both Syria and Iraq, and they resented Syrian support for Kurdish guerilla activities on Turkish soil and for Armenian anti-Turkish movements. Iran had a long-running border dispute with Iraq and a rivalry with Saudi Arabia over hegemony in the Persian Gulf.

Cooperative, bilateral intelligence relations with Iran and, separately, Turkey, took form in 1956–1958 through a series of meetings in Europe,

Ankara, and Tehran and then culminated in the Trident triangular pact linking the Mossad, the Turkish National Security Service, and the Iranian Savak, which was formalized in 1958. In the case of Turkey, agreement on the
pact was reached in a secret meeting in Ankara between Israeli Prime Minister David Ben Gurion and Turkish Prime Minister Adnan Menderes on August 29, 1958. This was barely a month after the July 14 Qassem revolution
in Iraq brought an end to the Hashemite monarchy there and moved Iraq out
of CENTO (the Central Eastern Treaty Organization, formed in 1955, during
the Cold War, by the United Kingdom, Turkey, Pakistan, Iran, and Iraq) and
into the pro-Soviet Arab radical camp. [11]

At the first triangular meeting, held in Turkey in late September–early
October 1958, the participants—heads of their respective intelligence organizations—established an impressive array of cooperative intelligence ven-
tures and even subversion projects that were directed against Nasserist and
Soviet influence throughout the region. They divided the Middle East into
zones of responsibility: Iran, for example, was to take charge of the Persian
Gulf, Iraq, and Morocco. [12]

Early on, both Ankara and Tehran fell back on temporary downgrades in
relations with Israel whenever Arab pressure became problematic. Both Turkey and Iran could allow themselves to offend Israeli sensibilities on a host
of diplomatic and public issues, presumably because they assessed that Israel
needed secret ties with them much more than they needed Israel. Thus while
Trident flourished quietly, the Turks raised and lowered the profile of their
overt relationship with Israel in accordance with their sensitivity to Arab
pressures over the Palestinian issue, Israeli acts of annexation in East Jerusalem and the Golan Heights, and related affairs. [13] During both the 1967 and
1973 Arab–Israel wars, Turkey refused to allow US military resupply efforts
for Israel to use Turkish bases or airspace. [14] In 1975, Ankara even voted for
the "Zionism is racism" resolution in the UN General Assembly; in 1991,
when the resolution was revoked, Turkey abstained. Even when Turkey finally raised relations with Israel to ambassadorial level in 1991—long after
Trident—it "balanced" this by recognizing the Palestine Liberation Organization (PLO) as a state.

Beyond the formal twice-yearly trilateral meetings, which rotated among
the countries and featured considerable socializing and exchange of gifts in
addition to sharing of regional intelligence assessments, Trident comprised
almost daily sharing of raw intelligence data. The binational Israeli–Iranian
aspect of the trilateral relationship was generally more active than the Israeli–Turkish dimension was. Iraqi Jews who fled the Baghdad regime to Iraqi
Kurdistan were then able to migrate to Israel and elsewhere via Iran. Israeli
officers trained Iranian forces, and Israel sold arms to Iran. In 1958, in an
early example of bilateral cooperation, Iran supplied weapons via Israel to
conservative Shi'ite clans in southern Lebanon. [15] Israel's collection skills

were often more developed than those of its partners, and in the case of Iran it virtually created a national collection agency aimed at Iraq and Nasserist subversion in the Arab-populated southern Iranian province of Khuzestan. The Israeli–Iranian relationship was also fortified by a dimension lacking in the Israeli–Turkish link: a joint interest, until 1975, in promoting the Kurdish cause in northern Iraq.[16]

On the other hand, at one point in 1959 the Israeli and Turkish army leaders met at the highest level in Istanbul (Israel was represented by IDF Chief of Staff Haim Laskov) to plan a joint military campaign against Syria, which never took place.[17] There were no trilateral covert operations.[18]

## ISRAELI–IRANIAN RELATIONS AS THE SHAH'S REIGN NEARED ITS END

From 1973 on, there were plenty of warning signs that all was not right in the shah's attitude toward Israel. We have already noted the manipulative manner in which both Iran and Turkey treated their relations with Israel, upgrading and downgrading them in accordance with the vicissitudes of their relations with the Arab world. Because Israel's relationship with Iran was more developed, involving the Kurdish project and arms and energy sales, it was also more readily manipulated by the shah. Thus, during the October 1973 Yom Kippur War, the shah joined the oil embargo imposed by OPEC to punish countries linked with Israel and of course cut oil supplies to Israel itself. He also, together with US Secretary of State Henry Kissinger, pressured Kurdish leader Mustafa Barzani to back away from his commitment to Israel to deploy his Peshmerga troops in a manner that would pin down Iraqi divisions that might otherwise find their way to the front against Israel.[19]

In 1975, the shah gave a revealing interview to Mohamed Hassanein Heikal, a senior Egyptian journalist who had been an intimate of Nasser. The interview was awarded a high degree of authority by being republished in Iran's press, which was closely controlled by the regime. For the first time, the shah openly acknowledged Iran's military and intelligence ties with Israel, rationalizing them in terms of Arab hostility during Nasser's time. "But now the situation has changed," he added. "Israeli media are attacking us energetically. . . . We advised Israel that it cannot conquer the entire Arab world. For that you need a population of at least 20–30 million. . . . Israel commands the attention of all the Arab nations. I'm not certain there is a final solution for the problem of this confrontation." The usually secularly oriented shah then proceeded to suggest a new regional pact involving Egypt and Algeria and based on an Islamic common denominator.[20] On at least one other occasion between 1975 and 1977 the shah, through his foreign minister, offered to Syria to cut all his ties with Israel in return for Arab concessions.

Trita Parsi, an expert on Iran and its relationship with Israel who heads the US-based National Iranian American Council, believes that at this point in time the increasingly megalomaniacal shah "felt that he had reached the top of the system. His policy was no longer to balance just the Arabs. His policy was to balance everyone, including the Israelis." Parsi relates a conversation with an Iranian diplomat from the shah's day, who argued that "Iran did not have Israel as a friend in order to have the Arabs as an enemy." In discussing the Israeli–Iranian relationship with Israeli and Iranian veterans of the shah's period of rule, Parsi notes "the lack of emotional attachment that existed on the Iranian side towards Israel . . . [whereas] from the Israeli side, there seemed to be not only an ideological [tie] but also a fulfillment of destiny. . . . This is a new chapter of the Bible being written. . . . And when you talk to the Iranians, they had no idea. They couldn't care less."[21]

Despite his statement to Heikal and similar ones to other journalists, the shah maintained his relationship with Israel. Oil sales were booming and so were arms sales. Several thousand Israeli businessmen and their families were living prosperously in Iran, serviced by an Israeli school and frequent flights to Tel Aviv. In 1977, even after Israeli Ambassador (in Israeli parlance; Iran recognized him officially as head of a trade delegation) Uri Lubrani had cabled home a warning that unrest was brewing in Iran, a secret $1.2 billion bilateral weapons project, *Tzur* (rock) was apparently negotiated, according to which Tehran would finance development of six Israeli weapons systems, including combat aircraft and according to captured US documents published in Iran after the revolution, a new generation of the Jericho ballistic missile and a long-range antiship missile. Meetings over the deal involved Iran's General Hassan Toufanian, vice minister of war, and Israeli Foreign Minister Moshe Dayan and Minister of Defense Ezer Weizman.[22]

## ISRAELI–TURKISH RELATIONS SINCE TRIDENT

After the fall of the shah and the collapse of Trident in 1979, and indeed, with the collapse of the periphery doctrine in general during the decade 1973–1983, Israeli–Turkish relations in both security and other spheres maintained their early trajectory of high and low points, which corresponded with Turkey's crises and successes with the Arab world.

After a low point in the late 1980s—at the time, senior Israeli officials invested heavily in rebuilding the relationship, including helping Turkey in Washington to counter the Armenian lobby—a major strategic upgrade in Israeli–Turkish relations took place during the 1990s, well past the Trident period. Spearheaded by the all-powerful Turkish armed forces, important deals for Israeli arms sales were concluded, and Turkish leaders visited Israel. The regional backdrop was major Turkish–Arab tension, which derived in part from Syrian support for the Turkish Kurdish underground party, the PKK.[23] Only the years 1996–1997, when Turkey was ruled by Islamist Prime Minister Necmettin Erbakan, offered a brief but prophetic interlude of civil–military tensions over relations with Israel. At one point in the 1990s, confronted with Israeli–Syrian peace negotiations, senior Turkish generals tried to persuade Israel to desist and support their confrontation with Damascus; the suggestion was rebuffed.[24] Yet these demonstrations of friendship did not prevent the Turks from reassuring the CIA that "the reason we are so friendly to Israel is that . . . AIPAC [American Israel Public Affairs Committee] . . . is the solution to the Armenian problem."[25]

Eventually, the advent to power in Turkey in 2002 of the AKP (Justice and Development Party), under Recep Tayyip Erdoğan, heralded the beginning of a gradual phasing out of the Turkish military's influence—the mainstay of Turkey's strategic relationship with Israel—leading to a radical downgrading of relations. This culminated in May 2010 in the Mavi Marmara incident, in which Israeli naval commandos, in self-defense, killed nine Turkish Islamists in international waters in the course of an ill-conceived interception of a Turkish aid ship headed for the Gaza Strip.

Erdoğan was promoting Islam-based ties with much of the Arab world and spearheading economic development that rendered Turkey a regional power with little need for Israel. He jailed most of the military architects of the close relationship with Israel. Even before the Marmara incident, a Turkish diplomat told an Israeli academic audience, "We don't need you anymore. . . . There is no more USSR, no more Arab subversion."[26] Indeed, so dominant was Turkey becoming regionally that once the Arab revolutions broke out in early 2011, Washington could ill afford to alienate Ankara—now a paragon of the kind of integration of Islam with democracy that the United States could only hope would emerge in Egypt, Tunisia, and elsewhere—just because it did not get along with Israel.

By 2014 Turkey's regional status had weakened, precisely because of Arab resentment over its interference. Israeli prime minister Benjamin Netanyahu had, with American intervention, apologized over the Mavi Marmara incident, and a new strategic equilibrium might have begun to emerge: Turkey and Israel saw eye to eye over the need to protect Kurdish quasi-independence in Iraq and possibly Syria, they recognized a need to coordinate at a fundamental level their strategic needs in a crisis-torn Syria, and they might be able to collaborate over energy issues involving eastern Mediterranean natural gas discoveries. In any case, Israeli–Turkish economic relations had never suffered because of the Mavi Marmara crisis, but the level of security intimacy developed during Trident and in the 1990s was gone.

As one Turkish businessman put it a few months after the Mavi Marmara incident, "For us it comes down to profits. For the Israelis, it's emotional."[27] Alongside the rise of political Islam, perhaps nothing better describes the difficulty Israel has had in adjusting to the collapse of periphery relationships, particularly with Turkey and Iran.

Some months after the May 2010 Mavi Marmara incident, which so thoroughly soured Israeli–Turkish relations, I had a cup of coffee in a trendy Ramat HaSharon café with Ceylan Ozen, counselor at the Turkish embassy in Tel Aviv. Since Ankara had withdrawn its ambassador to protest the incident, Ms. Ozen was in charge.

The conversation focused on the various commissions of inquiry investigating the incident. We were at complete loggerheads in our interpretation and understanding of what had happened and what it meant for our two countries' relationship. Finally, in an effort to give the interchange some depth, I reminded Ms. Ozen how close Israeli–Turkish strategic coordination had been under Trident.

"What was Trident?" she asked. I explained. She had never heard the name, nor had she heard, in fifteen years as a diplomat and in her two years in Israel, that Turkey, Israel, and Iran had once been partners in a strategic alliance. She was certain none of her colleagues knew either. She added that Turkish officials had been distressed when until a year earlier, Israel officials had termed the two countries' twice-yearly bilateral diplomatic meetings "strategic."

Since the Turkish military is no longer involved in the country's strategic affairs in any way approaching the scope of the pre-Erdoğan period, this means that Israeli–Turkish relations are today managed by Ankara more or less as though Trident never happened.

## ASSESSING TRIDENT

From Israel's standpoint, Trident was a lopsided intelligence alliance under a gloss of often pompous protocol: Israel provided far better information and more intelligence know-how than it received in return. "Lots of ceremony . . . it was almost pathetic how hard we tried like kids to give it the rituals of regular alliances," states Uzi Arad.[28] David Kimche adds, "It turned out the much-praised efficiency of Iranian intelligence . . . was very limited. It's astounding how shallow in vital areas their intelligence was."[29]

"They saw us as the oracle," Ephraim Halevy comments:

> We were the experts on everything, we supplied the intelligence on everything, we supplied the working papers. . . . If they had working papers they were very poor in quality and they knew it. Even the summaries were written by us . . . their contribution was minor. . . . I once asked Nafti [Naftali Keinan,

who headed the Mossad division responsible for interservice liaison], "at the end of the day, what was the value of all this?" and he replied, "its value lies in its very existence." That's the real definition of what happened. . . . The very fact that the three of us met was the symbol. . . . We [three] did nothing together, we didn't plan a coup d'etat in Egypt, didn't plan to recruit an agent, didn't run agents together. We had joint operations with the Turks and with the Iranians and the Iranians with the Turks. There was nothing trilateral. . . . There were never trilateral summits of heads of state or ministers.[30]

Despite its lack of real substance at the trilateral level, in the course of two decades Trident sent an important message to the Americans, the Soviets, and the Arabs: Israel was not alone; it had important regional allies. From the point of departure of Israel's acute isolation in the 1950s, this was of huge importance. It projected deterrence, permanence, and stability. The fact that particularly in the case of Iran, the intelligence relationship was supplemented by extensive civilian aid and trade only further aggrandized the impact of Trident in Arab eyes.

Nor is there evidence to substantiate the claim (see chapter 11, "Israeli Skeptics") that Trident interfered with Israeli peace negotiations with the Arabs. Indeed the shah, and to a greater extent King Hassan II of Morocco, helped facilitate Israel's contacts with Anwar Sadat's government in Egypt in 1977.

Trident's lopsidedness at the level of substance was paralleled by the gap between Israel's sincere belief in the viability of the alliance and the shah's cynicism. Israel was constantly and consciously looking the other way on this score, if only because it had no obvious alternative to Trident. This pragmatic approach often made sense from Israel's standpoint, as when a request went out to all the 1,500 or so Israelis involved in business in Iran, some two months prior to the Khomeini takeover, to continue dealings as usual but to make sure that at all times Israel owed the Iranians' money, and not vice versa.

Finally, Israel had made a tremendous investment in Trident and other aspects of its relationship with the shah, but Iran was not an open society and had a history of popular revolution. The scope of Israel's interests in Iran should have dictated a far more penetrating Israeli intelligence interest not only in collaborating with Iran but in understanding the inner workings of the Iranian opposition as well. Israeli intelligence was sophisticated enough to have been able to do this without unduly alarming the autocratic shah. Indeed, it might have been able to help him.

## THE FORTY DAYS OF SHAPOUR BAKHTIAR

On January 3, 1979, Shapour Bakhtiar's appointment as prime minister of Iran was approved by the parliament. He told the shah that the monarch must leave the country quickly if Bakhtiar were to have any chance at staving off Ayatollah Khomeini's assault on the regime and the country.

Bakhtiar was not the shah's first choice. Another veteran bourgeois opponent of the shah, Karim Sanjabi, had been offered the job back in November but turned it down under pressure from Khomeini's Islamists. Bakhtiar was even more secular. He was a francophile—fought in the French resistance in World War II—and an anticlericalist, even defining himself as an agnostic— an agnostic leader in an Islamic country: a "grand seigneur."

A little more than half a year earlier I had taken on the job of chief intelligence analyst for Iran. It had become clear that there was a "revolutionary situation" there: seemingly out of the blue one of the world's most wealthy, stable, and pro-Western dictatorships was in deep trouble. I had no experience with Iran to speak of beyond an earlier year of limited desk work and had never visited Iran.

I quickly discovered there was no one in the Mossad or the foreign ministry whom I could fall back on for deep understanding of what was happening. Yes, Israelis who knew Iran well had been the first to signal, a couple of years earlier, that something was brewing. Yet their entire orientation was geared toward the shah's regime. By stretching their capacity for creative thinking, some of them could get into the shoes of the "bazaaris"—the semi-medieval, semicapitalist middle class—or those of the self-styled moderate secular revolutionaries, such as Bakhtiar, but they had no tools for conceiving of the potential negative power, the popular appeal, or even the revolutionary operational capabilities of Khomeini and his mullahs.

The Iranian Shi'ite clerical establishment was a closed book to them. They had spent years in Iran without even noticing it, nor did anyone know Bakhtiar or his colleagues. All of them had been off-limits to friends of the shah, like us. The shah's own people—his intelligence, the Savak, and his courtiers—were all equally out of touch, so anyone who listened to them was deceived. Nor could friendly Western intelligence services help here; they were just as cut off from the emerging Iranian revolutionary reality.

After a while I understood that I enjoyed a certain objective cognitive advantage precisely because I never knew the ancien régime intimately, but that was small solace, as day by day the responsibility grew. In August 1978, after the firebombing of a cinema in Abadan killed nearly 100 Iranians, Deputy Head of Mossad Nahum Admoni phoned to ask me whether all Israeli civilians working on projects in Iran should be evacuated. I did not have a well-reasoned reply. I took a deep breath and said no, not to evacuate.

Almost by chance I was right. That day I was lucky, but I was already exhausted and the end was not near.

By January my mission was to assess Bakhtiar's chances. The real question was whether any of the narrow class of bourgeois antishah politicians of Iran, to which Bakhtiar belonged, had a genuine following beyond the twenty or thirty hangers-on one met in their divans, sitting around a large room in ornate, heavily padded chairs, smoking and chatting all day. Could Bakhtiar galvanize the army and the bazaar against Khomeini? Using Stalin's terminology about the pope—did Bakhtiar have any divisions?

For the next three weeks, Bakhtiar's situation became progressively worse. Khomeini's people in Neauphle-le-Château, his exile retreat near Paris, were becoming increasingly confident, issuing statements describing the Islamic republic that would descend upon Iran once the aging ayatollah returned to lead his homeland: Khomeini would be the supreme leader, or faqih, and he would "oversee the work of the president of the republic, to make sure that they don't make mistakes or go against the Quran." His aides at Neauphle promised eager US emissaries that the ayatollah would see to it that the oil would flow and the army would remain pro-Western.

In response, US President Jimmy Carter's representatives gave their blessings. Former US Attorney General Ramsey Clark stated, "99% of Iranians support Khomeini." UN Ambassador Andrew Young pronounced Khomeini "a saint." Pillars of the regime that the shah had left in Bakhtiar's care—the Savak and the army—were day by day declaring their loyalty to Khomeini and rebuffing Bakhtiar's orders. In the case of the Savak commanders this hardly mattered, since they uselessly continued to insist that Khomeini and his religious followers had no clout and the entire revolution was a communist conspiracy.

Indeed, at this time the radical left-wing guerilla organizations the shah had labored to suppress for years reared their heads and claimed for themselves the mantle of leadership. The Fedayeen-e Khalq crowed that it "did not oppose the shah's dictatorship in order to fall under an Islamic dictatorship." Moscow stood by ambivalently. To be on the safe side, it appointed the son of an ayatollah, Nur al-Din Kianuri, to head Iran's reemergent Tudeh communist party. Its propaganda compared Bakhtiar to Kerensky and Khomeini to Lenin. The Soviets, of all people, appeared to ignore another of Stalin's immortal thoughts: "Even a man with a box of matches can create havoc in Iran."

Most pathetic and least ambivalent of all were Bakhtiar and his fellow secular politicians. With bravado, Bakhtiar bragged that "it is the intellectuals, the political parties with doctrines, the doctors, the lawyers, the technocrats who decide a country's fate." When asked how he responded to Khomeini's demand that he resign, the prime minister replied, "I tell him— merde!" Indeed, bullshit was about the only ammunition Bakhtiar and his fellow bourgeois had. Another veteran politician said of a Bakhtiar cohort, Karim Sanjabi, "he isn't much, but his party [The National Front] has a great name." Mehdi Bazargan, who would be a puppet prime minister for a while immediately after Khomeini's takeover, stated bravely that "we of the Iran Freedom Movement believe in God and Islam but not in the clergy."

Everywhere, as almost always in Iran, rumors of foreign intervention abounded. And why not? Bakhtiar, like the shah before him, was constantly seeking advice from the United States, the United Kingdom, and Israel. On January 16, the shah finally departed Iran, carrying with him the disinterred remains of his father along with seventy suitcases.

In the midst of it all, it emerged that the shah was dying of lymphoma. No one in Iran and the world had known. Well, almost no one. In fact an Israeli doctor, Professor Moshe Mani, had been treating his cancer for years, but no one bothered to tell me.

Another astonishing discovery that emerged in January was the nature of Khomeini's revolutionary mechanism. It was run by the aging ayatollah by phone from Iraq and then from Neauphle to a certain Ayatollah Mohammad Beheshti in Tehran, who sat in an operations room equipped mainly with phones and tape recorders. Beheshti coordinated dates, demonstrations, and the distribution of Khomeini's cassette sermons and directed smaller operations centers manned by the clergy in Iran's other cities. That was how you made a revolution in Iran, under the noses of the shah and his draconian security apparatus.

On January 28, I was summoned urgently to the office of Mossad head Yitzhak Hofi, "Haka." Someone senior from the Caesarea secret operations unit was present. So was a unit head, a very senior operative who had served in the past in Iran and had presumably been called in for his reputed expertise.

Hofi opened the meeting: "Bakhtiar summoned Gaizy [Eliezer Shafrir, Mossad representative in Tehran] and asked us to kill Khomeini in his French exile retreat." Hofi was a man of very few words. He added something—that, knowing him, I knew was sincere—about rejecting the very idea of assassinating a foreign leader. He looked at me: "What's your opinion?"

Before I could even absorb the import of Hofi's question, the Iran veteran offered, "Let Khomeini return. He'll never last. The army and Savak will deal with him and with the mullahs on the streets of Tehran. He represents Iran's past, not its future."

Again Hofi looked at me. I thought of Washington's stand, Moscow's; the ramifications throughout the Middle East of success in eliminating Khomeini; the ramifications for relations with France and the Muslim world of failure; Beheshti's little operations room in a corner of Tehran. I took a deep breath. "We simply don't know enough about what Khomeini stands for and what his chances are to justify the risk," I stated.

Khomeini returned triumphantly to Iran on February 1, 1979. On February 11 he deposed Bakhtiar—exactly forty days after the shah had appointed him—and took control. Bakhtiar dropped out of sight and emerged after a few months in Paris, there to be murdered years later by an Iranian assassin. The few Israelis still in Iran, mainly diplomats and security people, activated a well-conceived escape plan on February 11 and got out. The rest is history.

In retrospect, removing Khomeini from the scene before he returned to Iran would probably have changed the course of Iranian and Middle Eastern history—although precisely how is impossible to say. Sometimes individuals matter very much in the fate of nations; we saw in 1995 how the assassination of Yitzhak Rabin changed the course of the Israeli–Palestinian peace process.

On February 17, Yasser Arafat arrived in Tehran to celebrate and took over the Israeli legation. Years later, I had a friendly chat with the Fateh Force 17 officer, a pudgy, studious general named Nizar Amar, who had sifted through what remained of our embassy archives following our hasty departure. Years later, I also learned that before approaching us, Bakhtiar had asked the Americans, the British, and the French to kill Khomeini and had been rebuffed by all.

Despite our intimate relationship with Iran and having been among the first to sound the alarm to Western intelligence partners that something was amiss there, none of us understood what was really happening. For Israel, this was the taste of a strategic intelligence failure regarding a major ally and regional partner.

## NOTES

1. Nahum Admoni interview, July 27, 2011.
2. E-mail correspondence, May 31, 2012.
3. Shabtai Shavit interview.
4. Professor Gencer Özcan, Istanbul Bilgi University, e-mail communication, June 4, 2010. For a detailed account of the Israeli–Turkish strategic relationship, see Ofra Bengio, *The Turkish–Israeli Relationship: Changing Ties of Middle Eastern Outsiders*, Palgrave Macmillan, 2004, 2010, ch. 2, "Days of Future Past—The Peripheral Alliance."
5. See Michael Bar-Zohar, *Ben-Gurion*, vol. 3, pp. 1322–1333, 1987, Tel Aviv, Zmora-Bitan (Hebrew).
6. Ephraim Halevy interview; see also Ya'acov Caroz, *The Man with Two Hats*, Ministry of Defense Publishers, 2002, ch. 8 (Hebrew).
7. For instances of US interest in Trident, see, for example, vol. 11, Iran students US embassy documents, V36-text.pdf.
8. See Menahem Navot, "He who seeks peace will prepare for peace," *Haaretz*, April 26, 2009 (Hebrew).
9. Doron Yitzhakov, presentation of doctoral thesis on Israeli–Iranian relations 1948–1963, the Iranian perspective, Iran Forum, Tel Aviv University, June 2, 2013.
10. Yitzhakov.
11. See Haggai Eshed, *One Man Mossad: Reuven Shiloah, Father of Israeli Intelligence*, 1988, Edanim, pp. 264–65 (Hebrew), and *Reuven Shiloah, The Man Behind the Mossad: Secret*

*Diplomacy in the Creation of Israel*, 1997, Frank Cass, London; Yossi Melman and Dan Raviv, *The Imperfect Spies, the History of Israeli Intelligence*, 1989, Sidgwick & Jackson, London; Israel: Foreign Intelligence and Security Services Survey, Central Intelligence Agency, p. 57; Ofra Bengio, *The Turkish–Israeli Relationship: Changing Ties of Middle East Outsiders*, 2010, Palgrave Macmillan; Ya'acov Caroz, *The Man with Two Hats*, Ministry of Defense Publishers, 2002.

12. "Report on meeting of heads of services of Persia, Israel and Turkey," in David Siman-Tov and Shay Hershkovitz, *Aman Goes Public: The First Decade of the IDF's Intelligence Branch*, Maarachot, 2013, pp. 94–95 (Hebrew).

13. Lecture by Professor Cagri Erhan of Ankara University, Dayan Center, Tel Aviv University, May 3, 2011.

14. See Suha Bolukbasi, "Behind the Turkish–Israeli Alliance: A Turkish View," *Journal of Palestine Studies* XXIX, no. 1 (Autumn 1999), pp. 21–35; M. Hakan Yavuz, "Turkish–Israeli Relations Through the Lens of the Turkish Identity Debate," *Journal of Palestine Studies* XXVII, no. 1 (Autumn 1997), pp. 22–37; Ufuk Ulutas, "Turkey–Israel: A Fluctuating Alliance," SETA Policy Brief, no. 42, January 2010.

15. Eyal Zisser lecture, Dayan Center, Tel Aviv University, March 2, 2009.

16. Nahum Admoni interview.

17. Özcan e-mail communication; Amir Oren, *Haaretz*, Aug. 4, 2000; Aluf Hareven interview, Jerusalem, Jan. 3, 2012.

18. Ephraim Halevy interview.

19. Declassified US cable traffic published by Amir Oren, *Haaretz*, Sept. 5, 2008 (Hebrew); William Quandt interview.

20. Kayhan International, Sept. 16, 1975.

21. Trita Parsi interview, Oslo, Mar. 9, 2011.

22. Iran students' US embassy documents; Uri Bar-Joseph, *Forecasting a Hurricane: The US and Israel's Estimation Record of the 1979 Iranian Revolution*, unpublished paper, 2011.

23. Interview with Menaham Navot, Ramat HaSharon, Dec. 26, 2010.

24. Conversation with member of Israeli peace negotiating team with Syria, Feb. 5, 2010, Tel Aviv.

25. Bruce Riedel interview, Washington, DC, June 20, 2012.

26. Menahem Navot interview.

27. Dan Bilefsky, "Beneath simmering relations, Turkey and Israel do business," *IHT*, Aug. 5, 2010.

28. Uzi Arad interview, Tel Aviv, July 17, 2012.

29. Amir Oren interview with David Kimche, Davar, on Friday, Aug. 21, 1992.

30. Ephraim Halevy interview.

## Chapter Three

# Morocco

Israel's clandestine ties with Morocco have been unique in terms of time span, scope, and depth. As an Arab country, Morocco offered Israel access to and understanding of the Arab world that no other periphery ally could provide. The Jewish element—mass emigration of hundreds of thousands of Moroccan Jews to Israel—was without precedent; it was also the link that preceded and helped pave the way for secret ties. The level of those ties, involving direct access to King Hassan II, was constant over decades. There was no other country in the periphery whose leader would credit Israel with having saved his regime.

Israelis were present in Morocco, facilitating Jewish emigration, before that country's independence from France in 1956. In 1963, high-level ties were established. They were suspended briefly by Israel in 1973 when Morocco reinforced the Syrian front on the fringes of the Yom Kippur War and again in the early 1980s when King Hassan II was piqued over a proposed joint operation. Even the spectacular defection and death of the chief Moroccan architect of the relationship could not damage it. It reached a high point in 1976–1977, when Hassan facilitated the Israeli–Egyptian contacts that led to the November 1977 visit to Jerusalem by Egyptian President Anwar Sadat.

## BERBER BEGINNINGS

Tel Aviv University scholar Bruce Maddy-Weitzman believes that an important dimension of Berber and Jewish influence in Morocco rendered it more likely than other Arab countries to enter into this sort of relationship with Israel. Berbers make up as much as 40 percent of the Moroccan population. "Berber militants . . . are convinced that they were once Jews. . . . 'Before we were Muslims, we were Christians, and before we were Christians, we were

25

Jews. . . . The Jews are the only ones who came in peace. Everybody else came as a conqueror.'" Maddy-Wietzman notes that General Mohammad Oufkir, who as head of the Moroccan security services was instrumental in creating the Israeli–Moroccan link, was pure Berber: "There was a natural intertwining there, I think, between him and the Jews and the king and the pro-Israeli stance." It is not out of character that the Moroccan constitution, promulgated in July 2011, cites Morocco's Hebraic and Berber roots and that the Hebrew date appears on the masthead of the French daily close to the royal court, *Le Matin du Sahara.*[1]

Meir Amit, who as Mossad head in 1963 spearheaded the establishment of the Israeli–Moroccan relationship, describes how he and his colleagues resolved "to exploit Morocco's problems to strengthen ties. . . . [T]hese had been based until then on the secret and special operations that had produced the major immigration [of Moroccan Jews] to Israel."[2] One of these problems, the Polisario Front issue, involved the territory of Spanish Sahara, abandoned by Spain in 1976. Morocco claimed and annexed part of it; the Polisario Front, a liberation front backed by Algeria and Libya, has fought the Moroccan claim ever since.

The exodus of Moroccan Jews also had been orchestrated by the Mossad through a dedicated unit (for more details, see chapter 7, "The Jewish Dimension"). It was an officer in this unit who leveraged an acquaintance with a Moroccan Jew who knew Oufkir into the embryo of the Israeli–Moroccan connection. Oufkir, it turned out, had grown up in the same region as that of a legendary Jewish sage, the Baba Sali, and was a firm believer in the latter's alleged miracle working.[3] Oufkir "was utterly disdainful of the urban Arab political and cultural elites, and would have preferred that Morocco not be a member of the Arab League"—seemingly the perfect candidate to run Morocco's links with Israel. Oufkir first visited Israel shortly after the relationship was formed, sent by Hassan in 1964 to observe the security arrangements for a papal visit, and became convinced that Israel could help him organize palace security in Rabat.[4]

As the relationship developed, Oufkir also became a figure of controversy. Amit relates how, in 1965, he had to maneuver to avoid too deep an Israeli role in the controversial assassination in Paris of Mehdi Ben Barka, a prominent critic of the Moroccan monarchy.[5] After 1972, when Oufkir led an abortive coup d'etat against Hassan and was killed, the Israelis had little difficulty taking their distance from him and were even falsely credited with uncovering the plot.[6]

## THE PARTNERSHIP IN ACTION

In late 1963, Israeli support helped Morocco survive its war with Algeria, in which the Algerian side enjoyed the active involvement of Egyptian military personnel. Ephraim Halevy, who served as Prime Minister Yitzhak Shamir's personal envoy to Hassan from 1988 to 1992, relates that Hassan credited Israel with saving his regime at the time. [7]

On at least one occasion, Israel sought to bring the Moroccans into a broader partnership with Kenya. In the early 1980s, Israel mediated between Morocco and Kenya to ensure that the Polisario Front issue would not embarrass Morocco at an Organization of African Unity summit in Nairobi. "We brought them to Israel, Moroccans and Kenyans," related a retired senior Israeli official. "I brought them both to [Prime Minister Menachem] Begin, who took one look and said, 'Wow, isn't this a strange get-together.'"

The Israeli–Moroccan relationship was known to the United States, which had military bases in Morocco and a close relationship with the king. Yet Hassan constantly sought to recruit Israeli influence in the United States. "In the eyes of King Hassan, we could deliver Washington," notes another retired senior Israeli official. France was also in the picture "insofar as it was impossible [for Israel] to sell Morocco French-made tanks without the agreement of the French government." Indeed, at the military-to-military level, Israel sold Morocco used French tanks and combat aircraft. [8]

Morocco's mediation between Egypt and Israel—perhaps the most significant diplomatic achievement of any of Israel's periphery relationships—began at the initiative of King Hassan II in the summer of 1976. His motive was reportedly concern regarding radical influence in the Middle East: Soviet inroads, Islamist subversion in Egypt, and fear lest the Palestinian conflict become more extreme. The clandestine aspect of what followed was heavily dependent on Mossad skills.

A meeting between the king and Mossad head Yitzhak Hofi led to a second royal meeting, this time with Prime Minister Yitzhak Rabin, who wore a blond wig to enter Morocco incognito. Rabin deposited with Hassan a series of key questions for Egyptian President Anwar Sadat regarding the possibility of a peace breakthrough. Another meeting followed, this time between Hofi and Hassan Tohami, Sadat's deputy. This paved the way for the breakthrough meeting between Tohami and Moshe Dayan, now foreign minister under Prime Minister Menachem Begin. To travel unrecognized, Dayan removed his eye patch and donned a fedora hat. People at the Mossad who saw his passport picture couldn't believe it was Dayan.

After the Israeli–Egyptian peace that emerged from these meetings, Hassan focused his mediation efforts in the Arab–Israel sphere on the Palestinian issue. This explains his hosting of Prime Minister Shimon Peres in July 1986 and of Rabin, once again prime minister, in September 1993. Incidentally,

Israel provided not only a clandestine link but also civilian aid in a variety of areas.

## NOTES

1. Bruce Maddy-Weitzman interview, Tel Aviv, Aug. 2, 2011.

2. Meir Amit, *Head On* (autobiography; Hebrew), 1999, Hed Arzi, p. 145.

3. Samuel Segev, *The Moroccan Connection: The Secret Ties Between Israel and Morocco*, Matar, 2008 (Hebrew), p. 134. Unless otherwise noted, the details that follow are from Segev's narrative.

4. Bruce Maddy-Weitzman, "Revisiting Oufkir: The Makhzen, the Moroccan Left, and the Amazigh Movement," unpublished conference paper, Aug. 2011.

5. Amit, p. 149.

6. Segev, p. 138.

7. Interview with Ephraim Halevy.

8. Segev, pp. 138–39.

# Chapter Four

# The Southern Periphery

In parallel with its pursuit of a "northern triangle"—the Trident alliance with Turkey and Iran, described in chapter 2—in the mid-1950s the Mossad sought to create a "southern triangle" alliance with Ethiopia and newly independent Sudan. Trident focused its intelligence cooperation effort primarily on Syria, Iraq, and Soviet penetration into the Middle East and only secondarily on Egypt. In contrast, the rationale of the southern triangle was mainly the capacity to project a presence south of Egypt and even—in Egyptian eyes—a potential threat to the Nile waters from the south while supporting Christian Ethiopia in its struggle with Arab Muslim subversion. Equally compelling was the need to secure safe Israeli passage in the Bab al-Mandeb Straits and the Red Sea, through which energy imports from Iran would pass to Eilat, Israel's emerging southern port.

In turn, these same strategic objectives informed a number of additional and generally successful periphery operations from the 1960s onward, which looked beyond the southern triangle: in the Horn of Africa, East Africa, South Sudan, and—east of Bab al-Mandeb—Yemen and Oman in South Arabia.

The degree to which Israel involved or even sought to involve the United States in its southern periphery activities was of minor significance compared to the northern triangle and the Kurdish connection. In contrast, British ties were important in the Sudanese, Kenyan, Yemeni, and Gulf contexts. Israel even worked with international Christian organizations in southern Sudan. The Jewish dimension that was so prominent in the Moroccan and Kurdish contexts was preeminent in the southern context in managing ties with only Ethiopia into the 1980s. Prior to the departure from the scene of Emperor Haile Selassie in the mid-1970s, Israel consciously marginalized the Ethiopian Jewish issue in favor of strategic ties with Addis Ababa.

Nearly everywhere in the southern periphery, the pattern was once again one of improvisation. The scope of success was in some ways greater than in the northern triangle and the Iraqi Kurdish connection.

## ETHIOPIA AND SUDAN

The southern triangle would prove less robust and resilient than would Trident. Trilateral Israeli–Ethiopian–Sudanese clandestine consultations were never held. The Sudanese leadership, which initiated ties in 1954 through British intermediaries while still under British–Egyptian rule, gained independence in 1956 and dropped out of the alliance after a coup d'etat in 1958, cutting Khartoum's clandestine ties with Israel.[1] In July 1957 an attempt was made to arrange a meeting between Prime Minister Ben Gurion and his Sudanese counterpart, apparently without result.[2] A tentative link would be renewed briefly in 1984–1985, when contacts with Sudanese officials enabled Israel to establish a presence aimed at facilitating immigration to Israel of Ethiopian Jews via Sudan.

Ties with Ethiopia would prove more lasting and involved close security and intelligence cooperation as well as assistance in agriculture, education, and other civilian fields, until a break in diplomatic relations after the 1973 Yom Kippur War (following the lead of many African countries) and a reduction in clandestine links during the years following the fall of Emperor Haile Selassie in 1974. At its peak in the 1960s and early 1970s, the size of Israel's aid delegation in Addis Ababa, with families, was deemed sufficient to support one of the few Israeli schools maintained abroad. The Israel Defense Forces (IDF) trained key units in the Ethiopian armed forces, and Israeli security operatives advised the emperor's security personnel. The Israeli military presence even survived a coup attempt by Ethiopian officers it had trained. In fact, Israelis in Ethiopia trained not only Ethiopians, but at one point in 1962, Israel reportedly trained Nelson Mandela, then a young South African revolutionary using an assumed name, in sabotage and weaponry.[3]

Throughout, the issue of immigration to Israel by Ethiopian Jewry was deliberately downplayed by Israel, lest it interfere with the strategic relationship, and because no Israeli leader was prepared to deal with the domestic politics of confirming the Jewish status of the black Ethiopian Jews until Menachem Begin became prime minister in 1977.

At least one head of Mossad, who had also served in Ethiopia, recalls Israeli–Ethiopian ties as being based on Christian Ethiopia's fears of its Muslim neighbors as well as the biblical link based on King Solomon and the Queen of Sheba.[4]

In Israeli thinking, there was an obvious commonality between ties with Iran/Persia, which go back as far as Queen Esther and the Purim story, and ties with Ethiopia, with roots traceable, at least in the eyes of Ethiopian Christians, to the Queen of Sheba. In effect, the Ethiopian periphery link was part and parcel of a process whereby the region's pre–Arab era peoples were seemingly drawn toward one another.

Ties between the prestate Yishuv and Ethiopia began in the 1920s; Jewish doctors from Mandatory Palestine served under the British army in Ethiopia during World War II. Israelis and other Jews could not but note the deep roots of Ethiopian Christianity in the Old Testament and in biblical practices, such as eighth-day circumcision. Haile Selassie was welcomed by the Jews of Jerusalem when he sought asylum there in 1936, fleeing from invasion by Mussolini's forces. The dynamic British officer Orde Wingate—a Christian Zionist who helped train Jewish resistance units in Palestine to fight Arab attacks in the late 1930s and went on to lead Haile Selassie's forces alongside British units that expelled the Italians from Ethiopia in 1941—championed relations between the Ethiopians and the Jews.

Yet at the same time, like the shah of Iran and Turkish leaders, Haile Selassie's links with Israel were frequently ambiguous and opaque. He feared Arab reaction and occasionally seemed to believe that Arab leaders might offer a better deal. An anti-Semitic current in Ethiopian Christian literature might even have had a modifying influence on ties with Israel. In the UN in the late 1940s, Ethiopia—like Iran and Turkey—supported neither the creation of Israel nor its admission to the world body. De jure diplomatic relations were not established until 1961; even at the height of the relationship, Israeli diplomats were not invited to official receptions.

At times the emperor listened closely to Israeli advisers, and at times did not. Ethiopian security officials visited Israel on occasion, but without publicity; the emperor never visited sovereign Israel.

Ethiopian apprehensions toward Muslim neighbors focused on Egypt, which was understood as an antagonist due to Nasser's incitement of Ethiopian and Eritrean Muslims, Egyptian involvement in the civil war in Yemen and (after its independence in 1960) in Somalia, tensions over the Nile waters, and even disputes between the Coptic and Ethiopian Christian establishments.

Ethiopia's severance of diplomatic relations with Israel in October 1973 was part and parcel of a wholesale break by sub-Saharan Africa, which took place against the backdrop of the Yom Kippur War. Israel's foreign ministry had failed to appreciate the impact of post-1967 Arab propaganda, led by Egypt, portraying Israel as occupier of African land (Egyptian Sinai). In Ethiopia in particular, a host of additional signs had been missed or underestimated, focusing on Haile Selassie's decline and the spread of internal discontent.[5] As for the secret relationship, as in Iran, the ambiguities and dualities of ties with Israel had been plain for all to see but impossible to counter. Unlike in Iran, Israel did not lose economic assets as a consequence of the break.

After the emperor's death in 1974 and throughout the rocky years of coups and intrigues that followed, Israel continued to maintain at least a clandestine presence. At one point in the late 1970s, the nightly murders of suspected regime opponents—some dumped at the gate of the only remaining Israeli compound—by the new dictator, Mengistu Haile Mariam, became so traumatic that the clandestine Israeli representative asked headquarters to be allowed to return home.

Israel never considered establishing ties with Somalia, a non-Arab but Muslim state bordering Djibouti, Ethiopia, and Kenya, because of Israel's close ties with the latter two countries, including the supreme importance of enabling Ethiopian Jews to immigrate to Israel. Hence a visit to Somalia in 1980 was really of marginal importance in the larger southern periphery scheme of things.

## PING-PONG IN MOGADISHU

Somali president Mohamed Siad Barre spoke decent English but with a thick Italian accent, which taken together with his gruff appearance—but making an exception for his safari suit—reminded me distinctly of a mafia chieftain in a Hollywood movie. To add to the dissonance, as we sat and chatted in the garden of the presidential residence in Mogadishu, we were treated to the sounds of a Ping-Pong game on the adjoining porch. Full disclosure: I had heard that Siad Barre loved Ping-Pong. I was Ping-Pong champion of my high school, but I didn't get up the nerve to challenge him to a game.

I was the president's guest, posing as a non-Israeli to facilitate travel and avoid arousing suspicion in a potentially hostile Muslim environment. Siad Barre had dispatched an emissary to Europe to recruit Israeli interest in his faltering country, which in 1980 was bogged down in a war with Ethiopia in the two countries' Ogaden border region. Somalia's traditional patron, the Soviet Union, was now helping the Ethiopians. Our own relations with Addis Ababa had had their ups and downs since the demise of Haile Selassie in 1974 and the rise to power in a bloody struggle of Mengistu.

Ethiopia was by far the more important country geostrategically, and there were Jews there who would begin arriving in Israel in just four years, after walking for weeks from Ethiopia to Sudan. This was not a time to anger the Ethiopians without good reason. It was reasonable to assume that Siad Barre saw a link to Israel as a possible vehicle to Washington whereby he could plead his anti-Ethiopian, anti-Soviet case and seek military support and financial aid.

So Siad Barre knew whom I really represented when he asked me outright what I thought Somalia should do in its current quandary: to whom should it and could it turn?

I hesitated. I had already spent several days seeing Somalia. Everywhere I went—from the strategic port of Berbera in the north to my cockroach-infested hotel, the al-Urub, in downtown Mogadishu, a bare kilometer away from the presidential palace—I was treated rudely the moment Somalis understood I was connected to the president. Ugly clan rivalries were everywhere. When I asked to see Belet Uen on the Ogaden border, where Ethiopian aircraft had bombed and strafed just days before, the escort assigned to me turned out to be a presidential son-in-law, dispatched to mind me lest I fall under the influence of hostile Somalis. (It was from him that I learned that by chewing qat and drinking cola one could easily stay awake and alert for twenty-four hours.) At one point, as I approached the presidential compound gate in an official car, two suspicious sentries jumped to a combat crouch, cocked their AK-47s, and pointed them at me in a challenge backed up by a fierce battle cry that had me ducking for cover in the backseat.

Everywhere I went in Somalia, the poverty was near incomprehensible. I saw tens of thousands clothed in rags and dwelling in makeshift tent camps. Only in the presidential compound could I depend on eating decent camel schnitzel and (like Siad Barre's accent, drawing on southern Somalia's Italian colonial heritage) pasta and drinking clean watermelon juice.

So I already knew that here in the presidential compound, I was in an island of artificial tranquility in an otherwise troubled and schismatic country. Should I do the obvious and suggest that this state of questionable viability develop ties with Israel? That was presumably what Siad Barre was expecting. Yet this could jeopardize our relations with Ethiopia, which were sensitive enough since it had moved into the Soviet orbit, and it might put us in bed with a problematic leader in a problematic country. Besides, I couldn't know which of Siad Barre's advisers who were sitting in on our talk were aware of who I really was and how they might react to the revelation of an Israeli connection. No one in Israel had prepared me for this contingency. After a moment's reflection, I replied, "Egypt has made peace with Israel and engineered a dramatic rapprochement with the United States. Why not try President Sadat."

He did, for all the good it did him. He was chased from power in 1991, and Somalia descended into chaos.

## SOUTHERN SUDAN

Clandestine ties between Israel and the southern Sudanese guerilla liberation army, known as Anya Nya (the name of a local poison derived from snakes), began in 1969. Joseph Lagu, a short, tough Anya Nya commander, went calling on embassies in Kampala and Nairobi in search of support for the south's struggle against a policy of exploitation and barbarity executed by the regime of Jaafar Numeiry in Khartoum. The case he presented was a classic centuries-old story of Arabs oppressing black Africans; in the instance of Sudan, the oppression was within a country that received independence from a British–Egyptian condominium in 1956. As an internal affair, it was seemingly safe from outside African, Arab, or other intervention.

As with the Iraqi Kurds and Lebanese Maronites, Lagu's quest involved an Arab world ethnic or religious minority seeking our help, unsolicited. It brought him to Israel and produced a first Israeli mission to his base at Owiny Kibul in the south, not far from the border with Uganda. Lagu was from the Madi, a minor tribe whose Ugandan branch included Idi Amin, then army chief of staff and later, when president, reputed cannibal and Africa's unchallenged buffoon. During the southern Sudan operation Amin's presence turned out to be fortunate, insofar as it facilitated Ugandan readiness to cooperate with Israel's aid effort and serve as a logistics base.

The first Israeli mission, like nearly all its successors in the course of the next three years, was led by David Ben Uziel, a former IDF paratroop officer with a rich background of working in Africa and a genuine predisposition to things African. Ben Uziel, known in Israel to one and all as "Tarzan" (after rescuing a child from drowning when he served in the early 1950s in the legendary 101 commando unit under Ariel Sharon) and in southern Sudan as "John," describes that first mission:

> The entry into southern Sudan was to territory that no one in Israel or in Israeli academia had a clue about. We had no idea what was really happening on the ground. . . . This was a territory cut off from God and man. . . . We saw skeleton children, we saw shattered villages, we heard their stories. The picture that emerged was of blacks who have no right to exist other than becoming slaves. In other words, the northerners could come in and do whatever they wanted. No one in the world was interested. The slave trade was supposed to have ended long ago. So what happened there did not preoccupy the world.[6]

No one even knew how many southern Sudanese there were in Sudan's south: probably around three million, with additional hundreds of thousands scattered in exile. Ben Uziel's description echoes the words attributed to British Prime Minister Lord Salisbury in 1897: "It is, of course, as difficult to judge what is going on in the Upper Nile [southern Sudan] as it is to judge what is going on on the other side of the moon." Yet Israel's ensuing decision to help the southern Sudanese fight Khartoum was informed not only by the mystery of the place and a genuine humanitarian concern but also, as with the Kurds of northern Iraq, by considerations of realpolitik.

Then Mossad head Zvi Zamir: "Before we set out to help them, we had to inquire how this step would be received by the neighbors." Zamir recruited the allegiance of Kenya, Uganda, and Ethiopia to Israel's southern Sudan project and then persuaded Prime Minister Golda Meir by exposing her to Lagu in person and his description of the horrific conditions in the south, where his fighters were using bows and arrows and spears against the Sudanese army. Zamir also calculated that a stronger fighting force in southern Sudan would reduce the Sudanese threat against Israel at the Suez Canal front and in the Red Sea.[7]

Then too, Zamir believed that a successful rebellion in southern Sudan would ease Kenyan and Ethiopian fears of Sudan's military power. Sudan was at the time aiding the Eritrean secession struggle against Ethiopia. Yet Israel's objective in southern Sudan was ostensibly modest. In Ben Uziel's understanding, it was limited to generating a rebel force that could harass Sudanese army garrisons in the south—creating "a factor that could not be ignored."

A further objective was offered by a then senior Mossad official. The Anya Nya could be deployed to create in Egyptian eyes the illusion of a threat to the waters of the White Nile, which flowed on to Egypt. Its operations would signal Egypt that Israel had "vertically outflanked" it and that "we are in the way." True, then as now, diverting or blocking the Nile waters flowing through southern Sudan on their way to Egypt was virtually a geostrategic and engineering impossibility and was never considered by Israel. But as we shall see when we look at Arab reactions to Israel's periphery doctrine (chapter 14), Egypt tends to take extremely seriously even a totally unrealistic and unsubstantiated threat to the Nile flow—its national lifeline.

All this was to be achieved through the presence of a series of tiny three-man Israeli task forces deployed for long periods in the south. The Israelis under Ben Uziel trained a southern Sudanese military force, arranged for weapons and materiel to be dropped by Israeli Air Force planes flying directly from Israel via the Red Sea and Ethiopia, and presided over a goodwill effort embodied in an Israeli medical team and field hospital, which ministered to the ill and wounded and administered thousands of inoculations against smallpox and yellow fever to southern children.

The southern Sudan effort was largely successful. In 1972, Sudanese President Jaafar Numeiry, exasperated by his military's losses, offered the south autonomy. A guerilla effort led by a self-made leader from a minority southern tribe and assisted by Israel had laid the groundwork for a separate African state, free of Arab domination. At one point, around 1970, we calculated that the entire Israeli operation in southern Sudan cost less than the equivalent of a single Mirage 3 combat aircraft of the type Israel purchased before 1967 from France and deployed against Egyptian and Sudanese forces at the Suez Canal front.

One of the Israeli contributions to the southern Sudanese struggle involved a publishing project based in Tel Aviv. In 1969–1970 I was in charge of producing and disseminating, mainly in Africa, propaganda boosting the struggle of the Anya Nya against the Khartoum regime. I created a kind of bush newspaper and a series of pamphlets. Everything was produced in Tel Aviv and rendered as authentic as possible: I copied the idiomatic English, the typefaces, and the format of African newspapers sent from Uganda and Kenya. Reporting was based on the material Ben Uziel sent us from Owiny Kibul. Dissemination was by mail from Kampala and Nairobi, where thousands of preaddressed envelopes were sent by diplomatic pouch and then stamped and mailed anonymously to local newspapers, foreign journalists, and international diplomats based in East Africa. The idea was to boost the armed struggle in the bush by putting the Anya Nya "on the map," with no traces whatsoever of Israel.

There were three high points in my brief career as the Anya Nya's informal public relations director. One was a visit with Joseph Lagu at a base inside southern Sudan, where I could interview him for the movement's newspaper. Before we began the trek through the bush to Lagu, a short distance from our group's departure from Kampala northward to the Uganda–Sudan border, we stopped at the Falls Dam, situated at Jinja, where the White Nile flows north from Lake Victoria. There, standing on the dam overlooking the falls, one of our escorts, a soldier from the Ugandan army, regaled us in primitive English with tales of how he and his comrades would on occasion throw Idi Amin's enemies from the dam into the Nile, where crocodiles waited. He punctuated his narrative with frequent obscene "hee hee hees," which I have never forgotten. The scene reminded me of the descriptions of the barbarity of Muteesa I, king of Buganda, as witnessed by the early British explorer Speke in the mid-1800s. The déjà-vu scene was completed when I sat with Lagu, who rewarded me with a knife created by a local artisan in the exact style photographed by the early white explorers of the White Nile.

A second experience generated very mixed emotions. I asked Lagu's people to purchase crayons and paper in Kampala, send them with his emissaries all over the south, and give them to children suffering the ravages of war. This exercise produced horrific drawings of murder and castration at the hands of the Sudanese army. We published them, along with Lagu's description to me of the Anya Nya's struggle and the challenges it faced.

A third high point was ironic, frustrating, and comic. An Israeli diplomat stationed in Addis Ababa reported that at a cocktail party, his Soviet counterpart had handed him one of our "authentic" Anya Nya pamphlets with the comment, "Nice work."

The autonomy negotiated in 1972 after several years of Anya Nya struggle backed by us lasted ten years and then collapsed. The renewed rebellion that followed—this time without Israel's help, spearheaded by the centrally positioned Dinka tribe and aided by Ethiopia and Chad—ended in 2011 in the independence of South Sudan. Young officers trained in 1971 by Ben Uziel are now generals in the South Sudanese army. Joseph Lagu—first southern rebel and then vice president of Sudan during southern autonomy— now resides, at age 80, in Juba, South Sudan's capital. Israel's contribution enjoys a place of honor in the South Sudan independence narrative. Israeli satisfaction is diminished only by disappointment with the chaos and tribal warfare that have been South Sudan's lot virtually since independence.

## YEMEN

Israel's periphery-oriented activities in Yemen were unique in that they involved little direct contact with Yemenis. This contrasted sharply with Israel's experience in Iran, Turkey, Ethiopia, South Sudan, and Morocco and in contacts with ethnic minorities, such as the Kurds and Maronites. Beginning in 1964, Israel intervened militarily in the Yemen civil war (1962–1967) in collaboration with an unofficial but highly effective British effort to strengthen the royalist camp against the republicans and counter the support the latter received from Gamal Abdel Nasser's Egypt.

In Yemen, as elsewhere in the Middle East, Nasser sought to export his brand of Arab nationalism and Egyptian hegemony. The British sought to protect their interests in South Arabia and specifically their Aden protectorate and to blunt Egyptian penetration, backed by the Soviet Union, into the Arabian Peninsula. Israel's primary aim was to pin down and attrite Egyptian forces far from the Israeli–Egyptian front in Sinai. At the geostrategic level, Israel sought to ensure that a moderate regime in Yemen would avoid challenging its naval passage rights through the Bab al-Mandeb Straits at the southern end of the Red Sea. Fresh intelligence about Egyptian fighting capabilities and the Egyptian armed forces order of battle was a bonus.

From Israel's standpoint, this was a uniquely successful military support effort. Its end result was that Israel confronted a weakened and demoralized Egyptian army, one-third of which was still bogged down in Yemen, in the June 1967 Six-Day War. And it was an inexpensive operation: Israel Air Force (IAF) transport sorties over Yemen to drop arms and materiel were financed by Saudi Arabia through the veterans of the British Special Air Service (SAS); the Saudis may not have known where their money was going, though apparently they maintained contact with Israel via the SAS veterans.[8]

The latter, who recruited Israel's involvement, were based in London and Aden. From an official British standpoint their operation was "deniable." In parallel, a representative of Yemen's Imam al-Badr contacted Israeli representatives in Europe directly and was even brought to Israel for a visit. In Israel, the weapons supply operation was code-named *rotev* (gravy). Each of fourteen precarious supply flights, by an unmarked IAF stratocruiser taking off from and landing in Israel, lasted fourteen hours. Arms—booty taken from Egypt in the 1956 Sinai Campaign—were parachuted with pinpoint accuracy into valleys 12,000 feet high surrounded by even higher Yemeni mountain peaks that were controlled by the royalists. The first drop was coordinated by two Israeli agents infiltrated with the British into Yemen; thereafter, the British handled the logistics.

At one point, the IAF considered but rejected an air strike to destroy Egyptian planes based in Yemen as an act of deterrence and a gesture that might discredit Nasser. It's just as well this option was rejected; it meant that Israel's preemptive air strike against Egyptian air force planes at their bases in Egypt on the morning of June 5, 1967, would come as a complete surprise.

Notably, the royalist camp and Yemeni royal family who were assisted (without the knowledge of nearly all of them) by Israel in the Yemeni civil war were Zaidi Muslims, a branch of Shia Islam. The republican rebels, like the Egyptians, were Sunni Muslims. Back then, the Sunni–Shia split in Islam was not a prominent factor; the Sunni Saudis supported the Zaidis, too. Today, the Zaidi tribes in northern Yemen, now known also as Huthis, are near permanent opponents of both the Sanaa regime and the Saudis and have established links with Iran.

## OMAN

The same British SAS veterans who recruited Israel's assistance against Egypt in the Yemen civil war also brokered the beginning of what was to prove a long-term clandestine Israeli relationship with the Sultanate of Oman, adjoining Yemen on the southern Arabian Peninsula. Geostrategically, the Oman periphery relationship bookended Israel's relationship with Morocco at the far western extremity of North Africa and the Arab world, but its birth was startlingly different.

Sultan Qaboos bin Said al-Said ascended to power in Oman in 1970 by deposing his father. The British were closely involved in the plot, which involved getting Qaboos out of the detention his paranoid father had kept him in for six years. The father's *diwan* (court) chief, a Canadian named Tim Landon, confronted the father, Said bin Taimur, and told him to turn power over to his imprisoned son and leave the country. The father refused. Landon replied, "Don't you understand you have to do this?" "No, I don't," said the father, whereupon Landon drew his revolver and shot bin Taimur in the leg. "Now do you understand?" he asked.

The British, having witnessed Israel's military capabilities in Yemen and in the 1967 Six-Day War and wary of the political ramifications back home of their own involvement in Yemen and Oman in an era of decolonization, then proceeded to bring Israel into the picture. Israel's Omani connection was to produce a clandestine source of oil imports to Eilat and, via the Eilat–Ashkelon oil pipeline, for transshipment to Europe. After the Oslo breakthrough with the Palestinians in September 1993, Oman, like Morocco, would be one of the first Arab countries to initiate official low-level diplomatic relations with Israel—to be terminated several years later in protest over lack of progress in the Israeli–Palestinian peace process. Oman's hosting of the Madrid multilateral meetings concerning water issues in the Middle East, in which Israel participates, continues to this day.

## KENYA, UGANDA, AND THE ENTEBBE OPERATION

In the 1950s, Foreign Minister Golda Meir presided over a major expansion of Israel's diplomatic contacts to include some twenty African countries south of the Sahara. Israeli outreach to these countries included a great deal of agricultural and community-building aid based on the Israeli kibbutz and moshav experience of collective and cooperative farming in difficult conditions. In Kenya and Uganda, relations rapidly came to include intelligence and security cooperation based on the Africans' concerns regarding Palestinian terrorism and Arab incitement of the Muslim sectors of their population (and based as well, inevitably, on the needs of regime leaders to secure their own domestic rule). The ties with Kenya survived a wholesale African break of relations during the 1973 Yom Kippur War. In Uganda, on the other hand, in 1973 dictator Idi Amin severed relations with Israel and became a close friend and collaborator of the Arabs.

In July 1976, commando units transported by the IAF raided Entebbe Airport near Kampala, Uganda, and staged a dramatic rescue of Israelis who had been abducted by a radical Palestinian terrorist organization collaborating with German Baader-Meinhof terrorists. Idi Amin's new Arab ties had ensured the terrorists a friendly environment at Entebbe. The operation would have been impossible had the IAF not been able to overfly Ethiopia and Kenya and land for refueling in Nairobi, all fruits of Israel's southern periphery effort, particularly its aid to the southern Sudanese uprising.

At the time of the operation, I was attending an annual Organization of African Unity summit in Port Louis, capital of Mauritius. I was of course posing as a non-Israeli. My mission was to learn about how Africa worked, and particularly about the Arab role in the continent's affairs, which were then dominated not by Middle East issues but rather by the drama of Rhodesian/Zimbabwean independence. When news of the Entebbe rescue broke on the morning of July 4, I realized I no longer had to observe the pretense of being interested in southern African issues. As long as I made it my business to quote the BBC radio report on the Entebbe event, to note that it had taken place in the very heart of Africa, I could now inquire of the Arabs attending the conference as to their reaction, without arousing suspicion as to my motives.

Two responses were instructive. The Moroccan delegation cheered: "We knew the Israelis could do it. We congratulate them." In contrast the Egyptian delegation, which included several high-ranking army officers, was dumbstruck. "Impossible," they exclaimed. "The Israelis couldn't possibly do that. They are incapable."

When I returned to Israel and related this story to Mossad head Yitzhak Hofi, a general who had played a key role in the Yom Kippur War, he offered an explanation. The Moroccans knew us and our capabilities. The Egyptians still thought they had won the Yom Kippur War and had proved our impotence. Our ability to go deep into Egypt's African strategic depth and carry out a precise military operation was a rude awakening for them.

## NOTES

1. Yossi Melman, "HaSod HaSudani," *Haaretz* (Hebrew), July 1, 1979.
2. Ben Gurion diary, July 24, 1957.
3. *Haaretz*, Dec. 20, 22, 2013.
4. Interview with Nahum Admoni.
5. These and many other aspects of Israeli–Ethiopian relations until the death in 1974 of Haile Selassie are related in Haggai Erlich, *Alliance and Alienation: Ethiopia and Israel in the Days of Haile Selassie*, 2013, Dayan Center, Tel Aviv University.
6. Interview with David Ben Uziel, July 12, 2012, Ramat HaSharon. Unless otherwise noted, all further references to the South Sudan operation are drawn from this interview.
7. Zvi Zamir, *B'einayim Pekuchot* (*With Open Eyes*; Hebrew), 2011, Kinneret, Zmora-Bitan, Dvir, pp. 86–89.
8. The story of SAS and Israeli involvement is related in Duff Hart-Davis, *The War That Never Was*, 2012, Century, UK. Details were collaborated in an interview with former Mossad head Nahum Admoni, Tel Aviv, July 27, 2011, and by the author's recollections. See also Shimon Avivi, "Rotev beSalat Teimani," *Mabat Malam* 66, June 2013, pp. 10–13 (Hebrew), and Bruce Riedel, e-mail correspondence, Dec. 2, 2013.

## Chapter Five

# The Levant Minorities

The Jewish state in the making, the Yishuv, discovered the Levant minorities back in the 1920s and 1930s. At the time, there was not a periphery doctrine or even a periphery concept. Rather, there was "a framework of contacts with any Arab, regardless of denomination and demographic status, who would talk to [the Yishuv]. . . . The Weizman–Faisal Agreement of 1919 [an early attempt at Zionist–Arab dialogue between the leaders of the Zionist and Arab nationalist movements] was the most prominent, though futile, outcome of this search for relations." Early ties often took the form of transactions for buying land in Palestine from Lebanese Christian and Muslim absentee owners.[1]

Fairly quickly, by default, this search evolved into a minorities concept. Jews from the Yishuv who vacationed in Lebanon were discovered by their Christian neighbors. "It was the Maronite clergy who sought out representatives of the Jewish Agency and proposed the idea of minority-alliance."[2] Itamar Ben-Avi, son of Eliezer Ben-Yehuda, who pioneered the revival of Hebrew as a national language, wrote in the Hebrew press back in 1924 of the prospect for cooperation between Christian Lebanon and the Hebrew national home, which would lead to the day when "together we can extend our hand to Islam based on the complete independence of the Hebrews and the Lebanese along the shore of the ancient Canaanite sea."[3] Apropos Canaan, small groups of intellectuals in both the Yishuv and Lebanon promoted Jewish–Maronite ties as a renewal of ancient Hebrew–Phoenician links.

Cultivating ties with regional minorities was one way in which the tiny Jewish presence in British Mandatory Palestine, itself a minority, confronted growing Arab nationalist opposition to its plans for Jewish sovereignty. Over time, the ties would prove to be of a cultural, military, intelligence, economic, and diplomatic nature. This last aspect, the diplomatic, characterized the first substantive links more than eighty years ago, spearheaded by the diplomatic arm of the Yishuv: the Jewish Agency's Political Department.

During the 1930s, with the Political Department staffed by Arab-affairs experts (and future senior Israeli diplomats), such as Eliahu Sasson, Reuven Zaslani (Shiloah), and Eliahu Epstein (Elath), it recognized at least a theoretical potential to strike up alliances with the non-Arab, non-Muslim, and even non-Sunni (i.e., Shi'ite) minorities in the region, who also had presumed reasons to fear the rise of Arab nationalism—a phenomenon that was itself emerging to a large extent from roots in the Levant. The Political Department also saw in the Yishuv's relations with friendly minorities a way of gathering intelligence about the Arab world in general. Accordingly, the Jewish Agency looked northward: to Palestine's north, where the Druze of the Carmel and Galilee regions were to an extent friendly to the Zionist idea, and farther north, to French-mandated Syria and Lebanon, where a variety of Druze, Maronite, Greek Orthodox, and Shi'ite communities enjoyed diverse degrees of autonomy under French rule.[4] There is no record of significant contacts with Syria's Alawites, whose ancestral territorial redoubt on the Syrian coast north of Lebanon is not proximate to what was then Mandatory Palestine and is now Israel.

What would motivate Levant minorities to seek out contact with the Jews of Mandatory Palestine? On the one hand, there was a sense of shared hostility on the part of the Sunni Arab majority, based at least in part on religious determinations. Thus the Alawites, like the Druze, both of whom had split off from Islam centuries earlier, qualified under traditional Sunni Islamic practice as *rida* (reverse), meaning they had so distorted Islamic practices that their fate should be either a return to the faith or death. Christians, including the Maronites, at least were awarded *dhimmi*, or protected status, as people of the book. All were subject to inferior status by dint of the determination that "Islam is superior and there is nothing above or equal to it." Hence, at least at the theoretical level, these minorities would potentially be attracted to a fellow minority, the Jews, who entertained sovereign aspirations.[5]

On the other hand, Levant Christians, particularly the Orthodox, played a significant role in the rise of Arab nationalism and identified with Sunnis against the Zionist project. Levant Christians were among the founders of the Baath Arab Socialist party in both Syria and Iraq. Palestinian Christians would later play a prominent role in anti-Israel "front" organizations, such as the Popular Front for the Liberation of Palestine (PFLP) and the Democratic Front for the Liberation of Palestine (DFLP). Then too, anti-Semitic prejudices were embodied in Levant Christianity no less than in Islam, and probably more so. Moreover, precisely because Sunni Arab nationalism had many of its roots in Beirut and Damascus, many Druze and Christians with whom the leaders of the Yishuv met in prestate days warned the latter that the Lebanese and Syrian minorities had to make their peace with the Sunni Arab mainstream—hence were not candidates for alliance with the Jews—if they hoped to survive in the post-Ottoman age.[6]

Back in those prestate days, travel between British- and French-mandated territories was relatively easy, and Political Department emissaries were regularly dispatched from Jewish Agency headquarters in Jerusalem to make and maintain contacts in Damascus and Beirut. Ideas were floated for Christian and Druze "buffer" states or enclaves to the north of the future state of Israel, with the notion that such minority political entities could shield it from the hostility of Sunni Arab nationalism.

No such buffer states emerged during the prestate era, although the French colonial administration did experiment with the idea of creating Alawite and Druze autonomous entities in Syria. But the contacts developed during that time did nurture the notion in the Yishuv that the autonomy or independence of non-Arab or non-Muslim peoples elsewhere in the Middle East was potentially beneficial for Israel insofar as it would oblige the region's large Sunni Arab majority to acknowledge the right of the Jews, as well, to self-determination. The contacts even spawned a variety of schemes to catalyze the partition of Syria and Lebanon or parts thereof into their ethnic components, such as one developed in the 1950s (the "Lavi file") by Yuval Ne'eman, then a colonel in IDF Intelligence[7] and an energetic supporter of the periphery doctrine. (Neeman went on to a distinguished second career as a physicist and a more controversial third career as a right-wing politician who opposed agreements with the Palestinians.)

Two of these contact dynamics produced relationships between Israel and Levant minorities, the Druze and the Maronites. Ties with the Maronites led to tragedy in 1982–1983. The future importance of these relationships lies in their relevance if and when Syria, and with it possibly Lebanon, disintegrates under the weight of revolution and anarchy.

## THE DRUZE

The Druze link takes as its point of departure the Jewish–Druze alliance inside Israel, whereby Druze men serve in the IDF and Druze, who constitute some 2 percent of the population of Israel, regularly win several Knesset seats as members of Zionist parties, often giving the Israeli Druze community disproportional representation in the 120-seat parliament. In particular, given the relatively positive Israeli experience with the Druze, Israeli Druze contacts with Druze communities in Lebanon and Syria prior to 1982 repeatedly spawned Israeli schemes to link up with Jebel Druze, the Druze ancestral homeland in southern Syria, which enjoyed sporadic autonomy under the Ottoman Turks and French, and even with the Druze redoubt in the Chouf Mountains of Lebanon.[8] Notably, these schemes have tended to ignore the ideological inclination of the Druze throughout the region to shun the notion of a separate Druze state or entity.[9]

Jebel Druze has over the years been the most consistent focus of these Israeli schemes. As early as 1930, Zionist leader Yitzhak Ben-Zvi asked the head of the Jewish Agency Political Department, Colonel Frederick Kisch (a British Jewish Royal Engineers officer who had been recruited to the post by the Zionist leadership), to seek contact with Druze leaders in Syria through the good offices of Druze in Mandatory Palestine. This led to the Druze delivering intelligence information to the Yishuv during the Arab Revolt of 1936–1939. The Druze, for their part, apparently sought through the Zionists to improve their at times rocky relationship with the French colonial administration. At one point, the Zionist leadership entertained a plan for buying out Galilee-based Druze villages and transferring their inhabitants to Jebel Druze, using financial incentives, to make room for Jewish settlement in the Galilee.

During Israel's War of Independence, in 1948, elements among the Galilee Druze worked with the IDF against Arab forces. At one point during the war, an idea was floated by the nascent Israeli leadership to sponsor a Druze revolt against the regime in Damascus in the hope of reducing Arab military pressure on Israel from the north. Such a revolt, based in Jebel Druze, was indeed launched in 1954, without Israeli involvement, and proved abortive. It was suppressed so viciously by the Adib Shishakli regime, which then ruled Syria, that Israeli Druze briefly lobbied the government in Jerusalem to come to the aid of their brethren in Syria and a move was made for the IDF to train Druze volunteers for the task. In the late 1950s, too, IDF Druze units were prepared for parachuting into Syrian territory in the event of another Israeli–Syrian war.[10]

The Syrian Druze issue emerged most recently in Israeli thinking after the June 1967 Six-Day War, when Israel captured the Golan Heights (known in Israel until then as the Syrian Heights). While the region's Arab residents fled the conquering IDF, the residents of the four Druze villages there remained in place, in keeping with the traditional Druze ideological preference for cleaving to their land over their nationality.

The 12,000 or so Druze on the Golan were initially friendly and cooperative, and this encouraged Deputy Prime Minister Yigal Allon, a Galilee native, to launch a scheme whereby Israel would find a way to advance militarily some 70 kilometers farther east and link up with Jebel Druze on the Syria–Jordan border, thereby creating a Golan–Bashan–Jebel Druze buffer region separating Syria from Israel and, to a lesser geographic extent, Syria from Jordan. Typically when it came to Israel's nonsovereign minority friends, Allon recognized that Israel would have to be the prime mover in this endeavor and suggested seconding IDF Druze officers to the task. He also assessed that Jordan would look positively on an enterprise that reduced Syrian border pressure on it.

Allon wrote to Prime Minister Levi Eshkol proposing his plan in August 1967. Within days, the cautious Eshkol relegated the idea to IDF intelligence for clarification. It quickly emerged that the Golan Druze had leaked Allon's plan to Damascus, and Eshkol shelved it.[11] With the passage of time, Israel annexed the Golan Heights and obliged the Druze there to accept Israeli ID documents. This caused a major rift among the Golan Druze, a portion of whom declared their refusal to accept compulsory Israeli citizenship.

## THE MARONITES

The second dynamic is a complex of contacts with, and interest in, the Maronite community in Lebanon.[12] These contacts began with schemes launched by David Ben Gurion in 1948 and 1956, but not implemented at the time, to extend Israeli rule to the Litani River in southern Lebanon. The contacts proceeded with Israeli arms deliveries (some of which were carried out in collaboration with Iranian intelligence, with which Israel had just established links in the Trident alliance) to the forces of President Camille Chamoun during the civil war of 1958.[13] In 1978, in response to Palestinian provocations and attacks from southern Lebanon, the IDF did advance to the Litani, and in the resulting enclave that was created between the Litani and the Israeli–Lebanese international border it sponsored the presence of a local, largely Christian militia.

The culmination of these ties was Israel's First Lebanon War in 1982, which was based largely on an Israeli–Maronite alliance that proved abortive and ultimately harmful to Israel's interests. That problematic relationship ignored the warnings of Israelis who knew all too well the Maronite inclination to shift alliances frequently and precipitously. It also ignored a profound tendency among the Maronites toward anti-Semitism, which only added to the cynicism with which the Maronite leadership exploited its alliance with Israel.

Inevitably, the 1982 invasion also contributed to Lebanese Shi'ite animosity toward Israel. There had been sporadic contacts with the southern Lebanese Shi'ites during the 1950s, 1960s, and 1970s, including arms supplied in coordination with Iran to the five leading Shi'ite families in the south, who were a force for conservatism in the face of Sunni-led Arab nationalism. But Israel's status in southern Lebanon after June 1982 went quickly from that of liberator (from the Palestinians) to occupier—a mood capitalized on by the Iranian revolutionaries who helped organize the fiercely anti-Israel Hezbollah.

The main difference between Ben Gurion's schemes regarding the Maronites, which never went beyond the vision stage, and the war launched by Ariel Sharon in 1982 was that Ben Gurion yielded to wiser and more cautious advisers, who pointed out that many Lebanese Christians, including Maronites, opposed links with Israel and that Jerusalem had higher priorities than a Lebanese adventure.

An early expression of the debate within Israel regarding the Lebanese Maronites began on February 27, 1954, when Ben Gurion wrote from his southern kibbutz home at Sde Boker, where he had retired temporarily from politics, to Prime Minister Moshe Sharett, his successor, suggesting that the Sharett government sponsor a Maronite takeover of Lebanon. Ben Gurion, who feared Nasser's efforts to galvanize a united Arab front against Israel, wrote that "Lebanon is the weakest link in the [Arab] 'League.' . . . A Christian state is natural, it has a historic root and will attract support from large forces in the Christian world, both Catholic and Protestant. Ordinarily this is nearly impossible, first of all due to Christian lack of initiative and courage. But at a time of confusion, mayhem and revolution or civil war things change. . . . Without our energetic help this won't happen."

Sharett, who knew the Levant minorities well from his days as head of the prestate Jewish Agency's Political Department, replied a few weeks later in a pessimistic vein. He advised strongly against "trying to provoke from the outside a movement that does not exist inside." Were there to emerge "unrest among the Maronites aimed at separatism," he would not object to extending aid, even if only to cause "trouble for the [Arab] League." But were this to become known, as often happens in the Middle East, "it is difficult to estimate the damage this would cause us regarding both the Arab states and the western powers."[14]

Behind Sharett's assessment was the perception that while some Maronites were adept at promoting a separate identity from Arab Islam and at reaching out to the region's Jews and others for support, they would not themselves fight consistently and sacrifice their own lives to promote that identity. Indeed, they would switch alliances virtually overnight to maintain even short-lived external support.

The story of Israel's military adventure in Lebanon between 1982 and 2000, which commenced with a concerted intelligence and military aid effort beginning in 1975 and was spearheaded by elements in the Mossad and the IDF, has been related in great detail in countless books and articles.[15] The Israeli security establishment, confronting a divided, multiethnic Lebanon unable to prevent militant Palestinians and pro-Syrian groups from using its territory as a base against Israel, was itself divided between two camps regarding what course of action to adopt.

One camp, led by Defense Minister Ariel Sharon, IDF Chief of Staff Rafael Eitan, and elements in the Mossad, believed it was possible by force of Israeli arms to convert Lebanon into a friendly, Maronite-dominated buffer state offering a layer of security protection to Israel's north. Sharon had an additional agenda, too: expelling the PLO leadership and Lebanon-based Palestinian refugee community to Jordan, where they would "Palestinize" that country and thereby ostensibly relieve Israel of international pressure to accommodate Palestinian national aspirations in the West Bank and Gaza.

This camp was successful in winning the support of Prime Minister Menachem Begin, who knew little about the Levant minorities and, surprising for someone who suffered from Catholic anti-Semitism in his native Poland, tended to view the Maronites as allies precisely because they were Christians fighting Muslim Syrians and Palestinians. Begin bought into the Maronite leaders' warnings of a "holocaust" and seemingly believed Israel had a historic obligation to help them. Begin apparently also subscribed to Ben Gurion's prediction, which proved completely wrong, that an Israeli–Maronite alliance would appeal to the Christian world.

One element that seemingly captured the imagination of this camp was the ideological line of a prominent element among the Maronites that proclaimed they were not Arabs but rather Phoenicians. This approach conjured up an image of a Levant liberated from the Arabs and reconstituted among its biblical tribes: Hebrews, Phoenicians, Canaanites, etc. A US diplomat who dealt in depth with Lebanon at the time recalls, "The Maronites kept telling us they weren't Arabs, they were Phoenician and would speak Phoenician."[16] Needless to say the more outspoken and audacious among these Maronites, such as the miniscule group Guardians of the Cedars, were particularly welcome in Israel.

A second camp, comprising Mossad Chief Yitzhak Hofi, several of his aides, and many in the IDF, was skeptical of Maronite assurances and generally sought to limit Israeli involvement strictly to the supply of arms and training, without direct military involvement. It was not swayed by the lavish gifts and sumptuous banquets laid on in clandestine meetings in Lebanon by the Phalangists, a Maronite military movement modeled off European fascist groups of the 1930s. It was Prime Minister Yitzhak Rabin who set the tone for this camp's approach when the Israeli–Maronite arms relationship began in 1975 by insisting that the arms would be given for Maronites "to help themselves" rather than for Israel to defend them. By 1982, nearly $118 million worth of surplus Israeli arms and booty from previous Israel–Arab wars had found its way to the Maronite port at Jounieh and around 1,300 Phalangist troops had been trained in Israel.

What ensued between the Israeli invasion of June 1982 and the final IDF withdrawal of May 2000 proved that Sharett and the more cautious school of thought that identified with his predictions regarding minorities were right in this case. As Major General Amos Gilead, who as a major in IDF intelligence opposed Israel's Maronite adventure in 1982, stated on the thirtieth anniversary of Israel's invasion of Lebanon, "[W]e linked up with a non-existent partner . . . a gang of lowly charlatans . . . that deceived us into thinking it was possible to bring about a 'new order' in the Middle East."[17]

The Maronites' mirror image of that assessment was confirmed a few years after the 1982 campaign by Pierre Rizk, head of Lebanese Forces intelligence during the 1980s, in a conversation with then-CIA official Bruce Riedel. The Maronites, Rizk related, had manipulated Israel since the 1950s. The Israelis were naïve and foolish, knew nothing about Lebanon or the Arabs, and were desperate for friends in the Arab world.[18]

But toward the unhappy end of the Israeli–Maronite romance, the Maronites were also desperate—to keep Israel from abandoning their ill-fated partnership. In May 1983, I and six other Israelis associated with Israeli universities (I had left the Mossad two years earlier) were invited by Lebanese Christian professors to an academic conference held at the coastal resort village of Maameltein, near Jounieh in the Maronite enclave north of Beirut. The timing of the invitation said it all. It took place nearly a year after the Israeli invasion of Lebanon and many months after the horrendous Sabra and Shatila massacre of Palestinians in refugee camps, which had been carried out by Maronite Phalange soldiers virtually under the eyes of the IDF. Lebanese president elect Bashir Jumayyil, placed in office with Israel's connivance, had been assassinated by the Syrians. An Israeli–Lebanese peace treaty that had been signed only days earlier on May 17 was universally understood to be meaningless.

In short, the Israeli–Maronite relationship was by now in deep trouble, and this conference constituted a last-ditch Maronite effort to give it some intellectual substance. The nighttime IAF helicopter trip up the coast, lights dimmed and radio silent, and the heavy Phalange protective detail assigned to us everywhere we went in the Maronite enclave hinted at serious security concerns. When Professor Moshe Ma'oz and I decided to go for a swim at a Mediterranean beach across from our hotel, we were escorted through a sea of sunbathing, bikini-clad Maronite beauties by a phalanx of Phalangists wielding AK-47s. It was a disquieting experience: after meeting Siad Barre in Mogadishu, this was yet another Mafia-like adventure in the periphery.

Our Phalange hosts pampered us with gifts and a dinner on the ramparts of ancient Biblos, just up the coast, to the strains of "Hava Nagila." But an academic conference also meant the presentation of papers concerning Lebanon and Israel, followed by learned discussions, and it was here that the basic Maronite approach to Israel could not be concealed.

The Maronites' hero was Ariel Sharon, the architect of Israel's war in Lebanon, who was by now discredited in Israel following Sabra and Shatila and in view of Israel's growing losses at the hands of southern Lebanon's Shi'ites and their Syrian and Iranian backers. Sharon, the Lebanese explained, would push Syria out of Lebanon forever and restore Maronite political dominance in the Land of the Cedars. Every mention of Sharon's name generated enthusiastic applause on the part of the Maronite professors, contrasted with total silence on the part of the Israeli delegation, which included former head of IDF intelligence Aharon Yariv and Professor Itamar Rabinovich, a future chief negotiator with Syria and ambassador to the United States. This juxtaposition of Israeli and Maronite moods was punctuated comically only by Lebanese fawning over Professor Moshe Sharon of the Hebrew University, solely because of his last name and despite his insistence that he was no relation to the minister of defense.

Finally, the discussion climaxed in the emotional exclamation of one of the Maronite academics at the close of yet another harangue: "If you Israelis do not push the Syrians out of Lebanon, then we Maronites will have no alternative but to form an alliance with Damascus." We Israelis greeted this declaration with stunned silence. This was the Lebanese Maronite approach in a nutshell: there are neither friends nor enemies; you survive by exploiting an ally as long as you can, and then you discard him for a new ally.

## NOTES

1. Kirsten E. Schulze, *Israel's Covert Diplomacy in Lebanon*, Macmillan, 1998, p. 14.
2. Ibid.
3. Quoted in Uri Dromi, *Haaretz* book review, pp. 6, 8, March 2000 (Hebrew).
4. These contacts are described at length in Moshe Yegar, *The History of the Political Department of the Jewish Agency*, World Zionist Organization Publishers, 2011 (Hebrew).
5. Interview with Brigadier General (ret.) Shalom Harari, Institute for Counter-Terrorism, Interdisciplinary Center (IDC), Herzliya, Feb. 17, 2013.
6. See, for example, Georges Corm, "Lebanon: no 'civil war' this time," *Le Monde diplomatique*, Sept. 2006.
7. Shlomo Nakdimon, *Haaretz*, Aug. 26 and Sept. 2, 2011 (Hebrew).
8. See, for example, interview with Uri Lubrani, *Mabat Malam* 54, Sept. 2009 (Hebrew), and "Syria–Junblatt row and collapse of peace process revive talk of 'Druze state,'" *Ad-Diplomasi News Report*, in *Mideast Mirror*, Dec. 16, 2000.
9. Much of the following is derived from a Shimon Avivi interview, *Kfar Saba*, Aug. 23, 2011. See also Shimon Avivi, *Copper Platter: Israeli Policy toward the Druze Sect, 1948–1967*, Yad Yitzhak Ben Zvi, 2007 (Hebrew).
10. Avner Azulai interview, Dec. 29, 2011.
11. "Druzia," *Haaretz*, Oct. 15, 2010 (English and Hebrew).
12. For a comprehensive survey, see Laura Zittrain Eisenberg, "Do good fences make good neighbors: Israel and Lebanon after the withdrawal," *MERIA Journal*, vol. 4, no. 3, Sept. 2000.
13. Interviews with David Kimche, Avner Azulai, and Ephraim Halevy. See also Shimon Shiffer, *Yedioth Ahronoth* weekly supplement, June 1, 2012 (Hebrew).
14. Moshe Sharett diaries, *Sifriat Maariv*, 1978, pp. 2398–2400 (Hebrew).
15. See, for example, Zeev Schiff and Ehud Yaari, *Israel's Lebanon War*, Simon and Schuster, 1984.
16. Interview with retired senior American diplomat, July 30, 2009, Herzliya.
17. *Ruach Tzevet* 103, Sept. 2012 (Hebrew).
18. Bruce Riedel interview and e-mail correspondence, June 29, 2012.

## Chapter Six

# The Kurds of Northern Iraq

The story of Israel's clandestine relationship with the Kurds of northern Iraq, like the narrative of Israeli aid to the southern Sudanese (see chapter 4), involves first and foremost a strong humanitarian element. As such, it constitutes a particularly emotional chapter in the periphery chronicle. When the Israeli–Kurdish alliance came to an abrupt and formal end in the early spring of 1975 and Prime Minister Yitzhak Rabin appeared before the Knesset Foreign and Security Affairs Committee to discuss it, one member of the Knesset said to him, "I presume our aid emerged from a desire to help a struggling minority," and Rabin, who was not known for his sentimentality, completed the thought, "because we're Jews."[1]

Undoubtedly, the Kurdish operation had additional important dimensions. For one, it was one of the lynchpins of the Israeli–Iranian intelligence alliance within the framework of Trident, even if Israel never shared the operation with the third partner in Trident, Turkey, because of Ankara's sensitivities over its own Kurdish problem. Then too, far more than the Anya Nya in southern Sudan, the Kurdish Peshmerga guerillas, led by Mulla Mustafa Barzani, had the capability, should they take the military initiative, to harass Iraqi military units sufficiently to keep additional Arab troops away from a war front with Israel. And because of Iraq's centrality in the Arab sphere compared to, say, Sudan's, the Kurdish operation was marketable to the CIA.

Like the southern Sudan operation, the Kurdish one had severe limitations. In southern Sudan, the advent of an autonomy agreement with Khartoum ended Israel's involvement in the early 1970s. In Kurdistan, the shah of Iran's reconciliation with Iraq in March 1975 led the Iranian monarch to end abruptly what was by then a joint Mossad–CIA–Savak operation and condemn the Kurds to a bitter fate. Interestingly and importantly, with the passage of time and after much additional suffering, both of these periphery minority allies eventually gained full or quasi-independence. Despite the absence of a direct Israeli contribution to that more recent effort, Israel's generally selfless aid and support at a critical time in their struggle is recognized in both the independent state of South Sudan and the virtually independent entity of Kurdistan in Iraq.

## FIRST LINKS

There are today around thirty million Kurds worldwide, of whom some five million live in Iraqi Kurdistan. The remainder are in Turkey (around fifteen million), Iran (six to eight million), and Syria (over two million), with small numbers in Armenia and the West. They were promised national rights by the 1919 Versailles Treaty, but have never achieved them.

Mulla Mustafa Barzani, the Iraqi Kurdish leader with whom Israel worked from 1964 to 1975, took part in various Kurdish uprisings against Arab and British rule in northern Iraq during the 1930s and 1940s. In 1946, he led a group of 3,000 Iraqi Kurdish fighters who provided the military backbone for the short-lived Republic of Mahabad, established in Iranian Kurdistan with Soviet support. When that effort collapsed, Barzani led his fighters into extended exile in a variety of Soviet republics, returning to Iraq in 1958 following the republican coup that brought down the Hashemite monarchical regime. From hereon, Barzani and his Kurdish supporters would find themselves alternately in conflict and at peace with a variety of Iraqi regimes and at times even involved in violent and Byzantine regime machinations in Baghdad.

This is where the Israeli connection begins. In 1963, Israel's ambassador in Paris, Morris Fisher, brought an old Kurdish acquaintance, Amir Badir Khan, to meet Prime Minister David Ben Gurion in Israel. Fisher had first met Badir Khan in Beirut during World War II, when Fisher was serving in the Free French forces. Badir Khan, now a language teacher at the Sorbonne, made the case for Israel to help the Barzani-led Iraqi Kurds, a fellow non-Arab minority seeking independence and fighting numerically superior Arab forces. At around the same time Meir Amit, newly appointed head of the Mossad, met in Paris with Dr. Mahmoud Othman, a key civilian figure in the Kurdish rebellion. "Dr. Mahmoud" described to Amit how the Kurds "didn't even have money to buy tea and sugar." Amit, shaken by the Kurds' humanitarian plight, convinced Foreign Minister Golda Meir to allot them $100,000.[2]

Amit also met in Paris in June 1963 with his Iranian counterpart in the Trident alliance, General Hassan Pakravan, head of Savak, and sounded him out about the prospect of an Israeli link with the Iraqi Kurds. "Pakravan's response surprised me. . . . [H]e said the Kurdish rebellion was a golden opportunity. . . . Ever since the Baathist coup [on Feb. 8, 1963] and the elimination of Qassem [the Iraqi leader since 1958], the Iranians were concerned over Iraq becoming stronger." Israeli aid to a renewed Kurdish rebellion therefore suited Tehran's purposes.

Amit and Pakravan quickly agreed on a plan of action for Israeli aid to the Kurds, in close coordination with Iran. One of the Iranian demands was to move Badir Khan, "whom the Iranians considered an old busybody," out of the picture. Pakravan agreed that the Mossad could organize military aid and public relations guidance for the Kurdish cause in the West, along with civilian aid, for example, in printing textbooks for near-defunct Kurdish schools and maintaining a field hospital for civilian as well as Peshmerga use.

(Savak chief Pakravan, incidentally, will be remembered as the man who convinced the shah to spare Ayatollah Khomeini's life in 1963 and allow him to depart for exile. Khomeini showed no gratitude: Pakravan was executed at Khomeini's order in April 1979, shortly after the Islamic revolution in Iran.)

The Kurds were already receiving limited support from Iran but had little faith in Iranian motives; after all, the shah of Iran had to constantly keep in mind the need not to incite his own Kurdish minority to renewed rebellion. Amit notes that the Iranians considered Barzani (after his extended stay in the Soviet Union) to be a communist agent planted by the Soviets to make trouble. "The shah told me in no uncertain terms: 'I want the flame alive, [but] I do not want a fire.'"[3]

The Israeli decision to help the Kurds was guided by a combination of motives. One, mentioned by Rabin in the Knesset, was humanitarian: as noted in the Mahmoud–Amit conversation, the Kurds' overall living conditions were abysmal. All Israelis involved were sympathetic to a struggling fellow non-Arab minority. A second was strategic: the stronger the Kurds were militarily, the more preoccupied the Iraqi army would be with them and not with Israel. Third, if properly handled in concert with the shah's intelligence arm, the Kurdish project could strengthen the Israeli–Iranian relationship. This meant the Mossad had to maneuver carefully to develop a relationship with Barzani's Kurds while working closely with the Savak.[4]

Here a word is in order regarding the schisms and betrayals that constantly confronted Israel's effort to help the Kurds. It was evident from the start of the Israeli–Kurdish relationship that there was a distinct lack of unity among the Iraqi Kurds themselves, with various tribes, rival leaders, and at one point even a son of Barzani siding with the Baghdad regime or otherwise opposing Barzani and his Peshmerga guerilla army. In the late 1960s, a major anti-Barzani Kurdish faction, which cooperated with the Baghdad regime, was led by Jalal Talabani, later to become Iraq's first president after the removal of Saddam Hussein, and its first Kurdish president ever. Also, the shah did not hide his need to manipulate the Kurdish rebellion for his own purposes,

culminating in his ultimate total betrayal in 1975. Back in Tel Aviv, awareness of this element undoubtedly mitigated against exaggerated enthusiasm
for the Kurdish project.

The first Israeli sent via Iran into Iraqi Kurdistan was David Kimche, in
May 1965. Kimche's mission followed an initial shipment of weapons by
Israel, along with Israeli support for a Kurdish fund-raising mission in the
United States. Kimche, who years later would be deputy head of the Mossad,
viewed his mission strictly in military terms: the Iraqi army was a candidate
to join a Syrian- and Jordan-based eastern front against Israel. If the Kurds,
with Israeli help, could pin down Iraqi forces in northern Iraq, this could
radically reduce any Iraqi military effort against Israel.

At the time, and despite the preliminary contacts in Paris and Israel, no
one knew how Barzani would receive an Israeli emissary. Kimche was allowed to volunteer for the mission—not carry it out under orders—and
traveled with non-Israeli identity. "We had no idea how [Barzani] would
respond," he relates. "This was the danger. Therefore [my Mossad superiors]
said, '[L]isten Dave . . . there's a danger here, we're not telling you you have
to go.'" Once Kimche arrived at Barzani's summer headquarters at Haj Umran, high in the mountains of northern Iraq, the Kurdish leader proved more
than forthcoming. "He took the relationship to another level," a strategic
level that even Kimche had not contemplated prior to undertaking his mission.[5] He showed Kimche a portion of the 35,000 square kilometers (a territory larger than the state of Israel) of Iraqi Kurdistan that his forces had at
that point liberated, at one point even bringing him close to enemy fire.

In contrast with Kimche's pragmatic approach and more in line with
Amit's initial response, Alouph Hareven, who was quickly brought in by
Amit to handle the Kurdish file at Mossad headquarters, addressed the Kurdish project "first and foremost in humanitarian terms."[6] Zvi Zamir, who
succeeded Amit as the head of the Mossad in 1968, adds that while Israel
"was interested in pinning down Iraqi forces in the north of the country in
order to reduce pressure on Israel in its confrontation with the eastern front"
and "we had to maneuver in accordance with . . . our line with Iran," when it
came to direct Israeli presence in Kurdistan, "the emotional tie was para-
mount."[7]

Shabtai Shavit, who headed the Mossad well after the Kurdish operation
ended, adds in a sweeping statement about the totality of Israel's periphery
ties: "The only beautiful aspect we displayed as Jews and Israelis [in the
context of the periphery doctrine] was our support for the Kurds for moral
reasons."[8]

Kimche was followed into Kurdistan by IDF Lieutenant Colonel Dov
Tamari, then commander of the Sayeret Matkal commando unit, who reconnoitered for three days to ascertain that conditions were right for a more or
less permanent IDF training and tactical support unit.[9] This paved the way

for the first of many six-month stays by select IDF personnel, led by Lieutenant Colonel Tsuri Sagui of the paratroops (see preface), and always including an IDF doctor.

What followed were years of limited military achievements against the Iraqis and at least two memorable visits by Barzani and Dr. Mahmoud to Israel, but also repeated Israeli disappointments when the Kurds' performance did not live up to Israeli expectations. On the one hand, with Sagui's counsel, the Peshmerga quickly registered a key tactical victory against the advancing Iraqi army at Mount Handrin, allegedly slaughtering an entire Iraqi brigade. And Barzani's forces undoubtedly kept a portion of Iraq's army busy along its Kurdistan front on a more or less permanent basis. On the other hand, during the two major wars Israel fought in the course of the Kurdish operation, in 1967 and 1973, Barzani refused to launch a large enough operation to pin down additional Iraqi forces and prevent them from joining the eastern front against Israel at a critical moment. (In 1973, Barzani came under pressure from both Iran and the United States not to do so; see chapter 8, "The American Dimension.") Amit concludes: "All our attempts to motivate the Kurdish leader to act more aggressively against Iraq ended in failure."[10]

The chronicle of the ups and downs of the Peshmerga's performance in Israeli eyes should not be allowed to overshadow Israeli–Kurdish day-to-day military cooperation over an extended period of years of modern Middle East history. As a young Mossad operative, I played a role from headquarters. One of my first assignments was highly doubtful: a brief look at a Kurdish request to plan the destruction of two dams in northern Iraq—an act that, it turned out, could have totally unacceptable strategic and international legal consequences. A second was to create unique ordnance that would enable a tactical rocket attack on oil storage tanks at Kirkuk. Needless to say, the strategic operation never happened; the tactical one did.

The year was 1969. Small Israeli military, medical, and communications teams had been rotated in and out of Iraqi Kurdistan every six months for several years now. They lived near Barzani's headquarters at Haj Umran, high in the mountains, in the summer and at a lower altitude in winter. We were in daily touch through coded radio contact. Headquarters took care of the Israelis' needs in terms of equipment, contact with families, and here and there operational planning. That's where my assignments came in.

In the 1950s and early 1960s, dams had been constructed in Kurdistan to tame the waters that flowed south from the high mountains toward the Tigris River, which runs through Baghdad. The Darbandikhan Dam on the Diyala River and the Dukan Dam on the Lesser Zab River, both in Sulaymaniyah Governorate, provided water and power to Iraq. The task at hand was to determine whether either or both dams could be blown up, what quantity of explosives would be needed, and what the consequences would be for both

Kurds and Arabs in Iraq. The actual planning of the sabotage raids on the dams would be done in Kurdistan by Barzani's Peshmerga forces.

I went first to the IDF intelligence library at the Kirya in Tel Aviv. It was run by the legendary Caroline of the couple Arnie and Caroline Simon, veteran immigrants from England who provided a good portion of General Staff Headquarters' English-language know-how at the time. Caroline found me all the pamphlets I needed about the dams, published by the British contractors who built them. These I took to the Tel Aviv headquarters of Tahal, the Israel Water Planning Authority, where I met with a couple of engineers whom I had clearance to talk to. I never mentioned the Kurds, and the engineers were seasoned enough to know not to ask. They agreed simply to talk shop about dams, no questions asked.

They assessed that sabotaging the dams would, depending on the season, flood Baghdad with up to a meter of water, killing and displacing masses of Iraqi civilians. This would be a humanitarian disaster prohibited under international law. It would also deny Kurdish farmers vital water for irrigation. We informed the Israeli military team in Kurdistan to inform Barzani that for humanitarian reasons the operation was not advisable. (Notably, the sabotaging of dams and flooding of enemy territory reportedly occurs today in Iraq's Shi'ite–Sunni domestic fighting.[11])

I then undertook my second assignment, which turned out to be far more practical. Barzani's Peshmerga forces could get close enough to the huge Iraqi oil production and storage installation in Kirkuk to fire rockets at it. The city of Kirkuk lies more or less on the border between Arab Iraq and Kurdistan, and its oil resources and overall provenance are disputed to this day between the two sides. In 1969, Saddam Hussein's regime controlled Kirkuk and its oil, rendering them fair game for the Kurds in their war with the Baghdad regime.

We could supply the Kurds, via Iran, with *Katyusha* rockets taken as booty from one or another of our foes in past wars. Our delegation in Kurdistan indicated that the only likely means of transport for the rockets and their launchers would be mules.

Hence the task was to design and produce a mule-portable *Katyusha* rocket launcher.

In those days, an IDF colonel named David Laskov, a graying, stooped engineer who appeared to be nearing seventy and was probably the oldest senior officer in what was in general a very young army, ran a unique little fenced-in compound, about 100 meters by 50 meters, within a much larger Engineer Corps base in central Israel. Laskov's unit was dedicated to improvising weapons and related gadgets that were required for specific missions.

In years to come, Laskov would develop the amphibious bridges with which the IDF crossed the Suez Canal in the 1973 Yom Kippur War. He would be elevated to brigadier general and would serve in the IDF until his death at age eighty-six—surely one of the oldest soldiers in history, and a very clever man.

I went to Laskov with the necessary requisition papers from General Staff Headquarters, to ask him to build a quantity of mule-portable *Katyusha* rocket launchers. Again, there was no need to describe the details of their use, merely the caliber of *Katyushas*.

A week later, Laskov invited me for a test launching at a firing range in the Negev. I arrived to encounter a mule fitted with a metal frame structure about the size of a bulging briefcase, looking more or less like an old-fashioned sled and placed on the mule where a saddle would be. In it was a *Katyusha* of the sort we were sending to the Kurds. Laskov demonstrated how the contraption could be strapped to the mule and then removed, placed on the ground, adjusted manually for range, and pointed and fired. I ordered half a dozen.

Within a month or so, Barzani's Kurds indeed used the launcher to light up at least one oil tank at Kirkuk. That attack didn't win the war but it was good for morale.

## EXAGGERATED EXPECTATIONS

Not only was Barzani's reluctance to launch operations that would pin down Iraqi forces at a time of Arab–Israel war frustrating for the Israelis, but perhaps more controversial among Israelis who dealt with Kurdistan was what Israeli military and strategic experts perceived as the Kurds' insistence on fighting, in effect, like Kurds, not Israelis. Here, as in southern Sudan and among the Lebanese Maronites, it appears that Israel's military experts had to learn a lesson in cultural relativity.

Thus one veteran Israeli combat officer and Middle East expert, who repeatedly led Israeli teams in Kurdistan on behalf of the Mossad and once trekked and reconnoitered the length of Kurdistan from the Iranian border in the east to the Syrian border in the west, noted that "[a]s long as you're around, the [Kurdish] trainee wants to please you, and the minute you leave he will revert to being a Kurd in accordance with local character and mentality. It was naïve to think that we could create here a new type of Kurdish warrior."[12] Hareven agrees:

> The greatest asset of the mountain people—ten thousand mountains towering above the clouds, every mountain a natural fortress, stable and steep, and between them narrow passages where a few fighters equipped with anti-tank weapons can block armored divisions ascending from the Iraqi lowlands. Their greatest weakness—poverty: poverty of means, poverty of language, poverty of organization and maintenance. . . . The Kurds knew how to fight well . . . in an extended and stubborn mountain partisan war, in small and irregular units.

Israeli efforts to train the Kurds to fight set-piece battles as standard military units failed repeatedly. Hareven speculates—in response to an idea raised by then Defense Minister Moshe Dayan sometime in 1967 or 1968 to deploy Israeli commando and/or armored units in the mountains of Kurdistan—that even such an Israeli deployment, which never took place, would have failed due to "the prolonged conditions of deprivation that prevailed in Kurdistan."[13]

The Kurds had their own exaggerated expectations regarding Israel's role: that Israel would fight and win their wars, both in the mountains and on the diplomatic field of battle. Frustrated with the limits of Israel's involvement, they eventually looked beyond Israel to Iran and especially to the United States, which played an increasingly central role during the years 1970–1975. All the while, all parties concerned seemingly ignored both the shah's initial warning to Meir Amit that he wanted a flame, not a fire, and Pakravan's initial explanation to Amit that supporting the Kurds was a good idea because of Iranian concerns about Iraqi military threats. Ultimately, in March 1975, when the shah and Iraq's Saddam Hussein reached agreement to end their border disputes and skirmishes and resume normal relations, the most obvious bargaining chip the shah could concede to Saddam was to close down the entire Kurdistan operation, a project that, after all, involved the presence of Iranians, Israelis, and Americans aiding antiregime forces on Iraqi soil.

Hareven sums up: "During the 1960s we were the main agent of support and in the 1970s the US and Iran became the main supporters with bigger demands and tougher confrontations. Ultimately, instead of delivering achievements [this] . . . generated Iranian military intervention in northern Iraq that caused, with or without American agreement, the entire project to fail."[14]

## POSTSCRIPT: WHAT WE FAILED TO UNDERSTAND ABOUT THE MARCH 1975 AGREEMENT

The Algiers agreement of March 1975 between the shah of Iran and Iraq's Saddam Hussein was understood in Israel primarily in the context of the shah's decision to sacrifice the Kurdish operation in favor of Iranian–Iraqi rapprochement. The main additional feature of the pact that attracted attention was the two leaders' decision to mark the boundary between them in the waterway known as the Shatt al-Arab in Iraq and Arvand Rud in Iran, along the thalweg line, or median course—an agreement that technically remains valid today, even after an eight-year Iranian–Iraqi war and a major revolution in Iran.

Apropos that revolution, the far-reaching ramifications of one aspect of the Algiers agreement that was to prove hugely significant escaped the notice of intelligence analysts like myself—not to speak of the shah's own advisers. Under terms of the agreement and as a benevolent gesture by the shah to his citizenry of Shi'ite Muslims after years in which Iraq had been closed to them, thousands of Iranians were allowed every month after March 1975 to make the pilgrimage to the Iraqi religious centers of Najaf and Karbala, which are sacred to Shi'ites everywhere. Najaf was where Ayatollah Khomeini had been living in exile and isolation for more than a decade.

Now, finally, thanks to the shah's misplaced generosity, Khomeini and his lieutenants could communicate directly with devout Shi'ites visiting from Iran. The pilgrims to Najaf returned to Iran with cassette recordings of Khomeini's sermons and revolutionary preaching. "From Najaf, Khomeini and his son Mustafa built up a network of Islamic revolutionary cells. Every mullah [in Iran] was [now] called upon to turn his mosque into a command and propaganda center to preach Khomeini's doctrines and bid the people prepare for revolutionary tasks: demonstrating, propagandizing others, and striking. If the shah's treaty with Iraq made this possible, a similar warming of relations initiated by Syria in late 1975 . . . included 'student exchanges'" in both directions, which would grease the wheels of Islamic revolution. [15]

In other words, the shah's decision to liberalize relations with Iraq, Syria, and the Arab world in general, conceptualized in his 1975 statement to the Egyptian journalist Mohamed Hassanein Heikal, "now the situation has changed" (see chapter 2), did not merely close down Israel's Kurdistan operation. It paved the way for the shah's own downfall, the end of Trident, and a radical and revolutionary change in the political status of Islam in the Middle East.

## NOTES

1. Quoted by Shlomo Nakdimon, Introduction, *A Hopeless Hope: The Rise and Fall of the Israeli–Kurdish Alliance, 1963–1975*, Miskal Publishers, 1996 (Hebrew).

2. Menahem Navot interview, Ramat HaSharon, Dec. 26, 2010.

3. Meir Amit, *Head On*, Hed Arzi, 1999, pp. 162–67 (Hebrew).

4. These and additional details are related in Nakdimon, *A Hopeless Hope*. See also Eliezer (Geizi) Tsafrir, *Ana Kurdi*, Hed Arzi, 1999 (Hebrew).

5. David Kimche interview, Ramat HaSharon, July 12, 2009.

6. Alouph Hareven interview, Jerusalem, Jan. 3, 2012.

7. Zvi Zamir and Efrat Mass, *With Open Eyes*, Kinneret, Zmora-Bitan, Dvir, 2011, p. 83 (Hebrew).

8. Shabtai Shavit interview.

9. Dov Tamari interview, Jan. 8, 2013.

10. Meir Amit, *Head On*, p. 167.

11. Ali Mamouri, "On eve of elections, Iraq's waters become weapons of war," *Al-Monitor*, Apr. 29, 2014.

12. Quoted by Vered Kelner, *Kol Hair*, Dec. 27, 1996, p. 57.

13. Alouph Hareven, "With a handful of Israelis in the mountains of Kurdistan," *Maariv*, Oct. 10, 1980, p. 17 (Hebrew). See also Kelner, *Kol Hair*.

14. Kelner, *Kol Hair*.

15. Joseph Alpher, "The Khomeini International," *Washington Quarterly*, vol. 3, no. 4, Autumn 1980, p. 73.

# Chapter Seven

# The Jewish Dimension

The periphery doctrine interacted with Israel-related Jewish issues in two ways: *aliyah*, or the ingathering of Jewish exiles from the periphery countries and their vicinity, and exploitation by Israel of the powerful image of global Jewry among periphery leaders to further Israeli strategic needs, usually in the context of Israeli–US relations.

*Aliyah* was a key component of Zionism that required reliance on clandestine means long before Israel's independence in 1948. After independence, the clandestine infrastructure that had facilitated *aliyah* was folded into the Mossad. The ingathering of the exiles may be considered not only the ultimate fulfillment of Zionism but also an Israeli grand strategy, insofar as generating a critical mass of Israelis was a key component of nation building that projected deterrence and permanence no less than the periphery doctrine itself.

## ALIYAH

The primary periphery operations that interacted with *aliyah* were the Iran–Kurdistan–Iraq triangle, Morocco, and Ethiopia. The Mossad also facilitated *aliyah* through clandestine means from Syria, Lebanon, Egypt, post-revolutionary Iran, and other countries that refused to allow Jews to leave, but that story is not part of our narrative. Moreover, in some cases it made sense for the Mossad to totally separate its clandestine intelligence ties from clandestine *aliyah* activities so that failure or a mishap in one would hopefully not affect the other.

*Aliyah* of Iraqi Jews via Iraqi Kurdistan and Iran involved a small number of Jews drawn from those who had not joined the mass migration from Iraq to Israel in 1950–1951. After the Israeli–Kurdish connection was established

61

in the mid-1960s, Jews from Baghdad and Basra made their way north to Kurdistan through subterfuge. The Kurds then escorted them to the border with Iran, where Israeli emissaries facilitated their transport to Israel (or anywhere else they wished to go; London attracted a large Iraqi Jewish diaspora).

Zvi Zamir relates the circumstances of the *aliyah* of the first Iraqi Jewish family via Kurdistan, when he headed the Mossad. In periods of relative calm between Iraq's Kurds and the regime in Baghdad, Iraqis from the south were able to enjoy the cool of Kurdistan's high mountain peaks and roaring snow-melt streams during the summer months. In this way, a Jewish student from Basra found his way to Kurdistan and then brought his mother and siblings. The family was escorted to Kurdish leader Mulla Mustafa Barzani in his summer headquarters in Haj Umran, 3,000 meters above sea level. The mother "upon seeing him, removed a gold necklace and offered it to him as a gift. [Barzani] refused to accept it and asked me later to give it to the prime minister of Israel, and I did. [Barzani] inquired where the family wished to go and the woman, fearing to say Israel, said to America. 'You're not going to America, you're going to Israel,' [Barzani] replied. 'This is the state of the Jews. There is no country in the world to which we Kurds owe so much.'"[1]

*Aliyah* from Morocco began under French rule and then continued between 1956 and 1960 as an underground operation. After 1961, international Jewish influence in Europe and the United States was used to ensure financial compensation for the Moroccan monarchy, "indemnities," and foreign investment—all in return for allowing clandestine *aliyah* activities to continue operating.[2] By the time Israeli–Moroccan clandestine ties were instituted in 1963–1964, the bulk of Moroccan Jewry had left.

Unlike the Moroccan case, Israel's periphery intelligence ties with Ethiopia long preceded the emigration to Israel of Ethiopian Jewry. The latter operation was delayed both by controversy within Israel regarding the eligibility of the Ethiopian community—which had existed in isolation for at least a millennium—to qualify as Jews and enter Israel under the Law of Return and a fear lest Israeli insistence on the Jewish issue compromise the strategic link. By 1977 Menachem Begin, a strong believer in Ethiopian Jewish *aliyah*, had become prime minister in Israel, while strategic links had in any case become seriously compromised by the fall of Emperor Haile Selassie and the emergence of the radical pro-Soviet Mengistu regime in Addis Ababa.

What ensued were two major operations to bring Ethiopian Jews to Israel. Operation Moses, in 1984–1985, rescued some 8,000 Jews from camps in Sudan, to which they had fled clandestinely from Ethiopia. An elaborate undercover Mossad operation was put in place in Sudan to facilitate the exodus, along with bribes to Sudanese government officials. In 1991, Operation Solomon brought more than 14,000 Jews from Ethiopia to Israel in the course of a single day. In this case, Israel invoked US Jewish organizational activity and Bush administration connections to persuade a tottering Mengistu regime to acquiesce.

## THE GLOBAL AND US JEWISH CONTEXT

Our chapters on Israel's periphery alliances with Iran, Turkey, Morocco, Ethiopia, and the Kurds have all noted the impression that a key reason for the leaders of these countries and peoples to ally themselves clandestinely with Israel was their belief that as Ephraim Halevy noted, "[Y]ou just had to press five or six buttons and all of America would report for duty . . . since the Jews controlled everything."[3] As we shall see in discussing the new periphery, in some cases the impression continues to be relevant.

Here we are on sensitive ground. The attitude of the shah of Iran or the Turkish military regarding Jewish influence in the United States and Israel's capacity to direct it in the service of their interests could be defined as anti-Semitic—or it could be termed mere exaggeration. Similarly, Israel's willingness on occasion to exploit that attitude for its own ends could be termed pragmatic or, alternatively, downright cynical. There were indeed times in the Mossad when loose talk focused on ways to take advantage of "the Protocols" of the Elders of Zion, a notorious forged anti-Semitic tract that enjoys wide distribution in the Middle East. Jews have become so conditioned over generations to spotting anti-Semitism that there was undoubtedly room here for mistaken impressions.

On at least one occasion, a periphery ally turned the tables on Israel and went directly to a Diaspora Jewish figure who was deemed more capable of delivering than Israel was. In 1969, King Hassan II of Morocco opened a direct route to the international and particularly US Jewish community by meeting with Nahum Goldman, president of the World Jewish Congress. Goldman was inclined to a more dovish approach to the Palestinian issue than Israel was and insisted on advocating it in meetings in the Arab world and elsewhere. Prime Minister Golda Meir objected vehemently, but in vain, that she "did not need a second foreign minister in her government." For his part, Hassan was impressed with Goldman and believed that in any case the contact could improve his access to US military and economic aid.[4]

All in all, the existence of the Diaspora—particularly US Jewish influence but also the influence of Jewish cultural roots in Morocco and elsewhere—appears to have added an important dimension to Israel's periphery alliances.

# NOTES

1. Zamir, *With Open Eyes* (Hebrew), p. 84.

2. Michael M. Laskier, "Israel and the Maghreb at the Height of the Arab–Israeli Conflict: 1950s–1970s," *Meria Journal*, vol. 4, no. 2, June 2000, pp. 11–12. See also Meir Kansu, *Jewish Clandestine Activity in Morocco: The "Misgeret" and Its Secret Operations (1955–1964)*, Hotzaat Irgun Pailei HaMachteret, HaHaapala VeAsirei Tzion Betzfon Africa, 2001 (Hebrew).

3. Ephraim Halevy interview.

4. Segev, *The Moroccan Connection*, p. 140.

*Chapter Eight*

# The American Dimension

We have noted that the birth of the periphery doctrine in Israel in the mid-1950s coincided more or less with the formulation of a second grand strategy, whereby Israel established close security links with a major power. At the time, Israel was to some extent coordinating strategic affairs and operations with Britain (in Yemen and Sudan) and France (Morocco) and briefly in the case of the October 1956 Sinai campaign, with both. A close strategic relationship with the United States emerged only after the 1967 Six-Day War.

Yet as noted in chapter 1, from the very conception of the periphery doctrine, and specifically of the northern and southern triangles (Israel–Iran–Turkey and Israel–Ethiopia–Sudan, respectively), David Ben Gurion sought to bring Washington into the picture and get the blessing of President Eisenhower and Secretary of State Dulles. From hereon, the Israeli–US relationship was linked in one form or another with Israel's periphery activities.

## IRAN, TURKEY, AND THE KURDS

Thus, Washington knew early on of Trident and the Israeli–Kurdish relationship and recognized in them contributions to overall US strategic interests in the Middle East. It also contributed to the costs of the Israeli military and medical operation in Iraqi Kurdistan; when, after his March 1975 Algiers agreement with Iraq's Saddam Hussein, the shah of Iran shut off Israeli access to Kurdistan, the United States provided a safe haven for Kurdish leader Mulla Mustafa Barzani. As we saw in analyzing Trident, the CIA station in Tehran followed the relationship closely, to the extent of writing reports on it that eventually fell into the hands of the Iranian students who occupied the US embassy in 1979. [1]

One additional and, from Israel's standpoint, very significant aspect of US knowledge of Trident focuses on the October 1973 Yom Kippur War. At the time, indeed since the June 1967 Six-Day War, the United States did not have an embassy in Cairo. Egyptian President Anwar Sadat, aware of the depth of Israeli–Iranian ties and apparently of US knowledge thereof, passed messages during the actual conflict via the Iranian leadership to Washington for delivery to Israel concerning his conditions for ending the war.

Far more problematic from Israel's standpoint was the intervention of US Secretary of State Henry Kissinger during the war, via US ambassador in Tehran and former CIA head Richard Helms. Kissinger directed Helms to advise the Iraqi Kurdish leadership, in coordination with the shah, that the United States believed the Kurds should not take military action against Iraqi forces as Israel requested during the war. So efficient was this channel that shortly after the 1973 war, Kissinger was asked by newly appointed Egyptian foreign minister Ismail Fahmi to request that the Kurds heat up their Iraqi front as a means of preventing pressure by Baghdad on Egypt not to move toward accommodation with Israel. [2]

The Kurds indeed did not muster forces during the 1973 war, thereby violating in Israeli eyes a prior undertaking to do so if and when Israel had reason to fear the dispatch of Iraqi troops to fight Israel along its border with Syria or Jordan. Accordingly, Iraqi divisions were sent to the Syrian front during the 1973 war. Some Israelis who were aware of the Kurdish relationship saw this as a major failure of the periphery doctrine: it was unable to generate significant strategic gains for Israel at a moment of supreme existential threat (see chapter 11, "Israeli Skeptics"). Moreover, that Kissinger instructed Helms to ask Kurdish leader Barzani not to intervene on Israel's behalf points to the negative side of Israel's having involved Washington in its periphery relationships. (That the shah apparently counseled the Kurds in the same vein offers yet another indication of the critical limitations of the periphery doctrine in terms of Israel's most compelling strategic interests.)

## THE SOUTHERN PERIPHERY

Israel was even less successful in marketing the Israeli–Ethiopian intelligence relationship to the United States, particularly after the fall of Haile Selassie and rise to power in Addis Ababa in the late 1970s of Mengistu Haile Mariam, who initially sought a close relationship with the Soviet Union. Bruce Riedel recalls that for the CIA, "the Ethiopian component [in the Israeli periphery context] was never that significant. . . . The real action is Turkey–Iran." [3] David Kimche relates that Israel tried to persuade the United States to support a strong Israeli–Ethiopian relationship in 1977, when Menachem Begin made his first trip to Washington as prime minister. Begin explained to President Jimmy Carter that based on Kimche's contacts with Mengistu, the latter sought to take his distance from the Soviets and the Cubans and with Israel's help, "return Ethiopia to the bosom of America." Carter turned Begin down; the administration could not understand how the Ethiopian question could be the first item on Begin's Washington agenda.[4]

A similar, albeit more subtle, clash of interests with the United States occurred earlier, during Israel's Yemen operation of the mid-1960s. Washington was not pleased with unofficial British involvement in supporting the Yemeni royalists against the Republican revolt because the United States at that point in time was seeking inroads with Egypt's Nasser, who along with the Soviets supported the Yemeni Republicans. The US approach changed only in 1965.[5] Meanwhile the Mossad, aware of US displeasure, apparently managed to avoid CIA knowledge of its relatively minor yet strategically significant involvement in carrying out aerial arms drops to the royalists.

## THE EXTENT OF ISRAELI–US COLLABORATION

Israeli–US periphery-related contacts took place mainly at the clandestine intelligence level. US ambassadors to Israel barely touched periphery issues. Daniel Kurtzer, who served twice in Israel (1982–1986 and as ambassador, 2001–2005), had "known for years that this was a grand strategy," but his work touched only tangentially on topics such as the Kurds and Lebanon.[6] The late Samuel Lewis (ambassador to Israel between 1977 and 1985) had similar recollections.[7]

Another former US official who dealt with Lebanon in 1982 when Israel, with Washington's knowledge invaded in collaboration with the Maronites, put the broad US role into deeper perspective: "I do not believe that the US, at any point in its involvement, was ever, at its own leadership level, fully aware of either the historical or actual political circumstances of the [Israeli–Maronite] alliance, the goals of the alliance, their implications for Lebanon or Israel, for the US, for the region"—all of which, he acknowledged, reflected both a good Israeli marketing job as well as lack of solid information in Washington. Israel's Lebanon operation, designed "to elevate the Maronites to the decisive group in the Lebanese polity, to eventually conceive of a government which the Maronites could direct . . . into a treaty relationship with Israel," was an "overstep by the Maronites, overstep by Israel, overstep by the United States." The latter, despite its relative ignorance of Israel's motives, "was a partner of Israel in this effort, starting with the summer of 1982 and the Lebanon War.

"The fundamental motivation for US support for this initiative," noted this diplomat, who preferred that his name not be revealed because he is still in active service, "had as much to do with US strategy vis-à-vis the Soviet

Union and the Middle East and the perception of what hurt or helped the Soviet Union in the region, as it did with the actual events taking place . . . in Lebanon."[8]

One notable and relatively late instance of Israeli–US cooperation regarding the periphery was the Iran–Contra affair of the mid-1980s, which will be looked at in greater depth in chapter 10. As former senior US officials with extensive Middle East experience recently observed, what is of interest here is the fact of an abortive joint Israeli–US attempt to establish strategic inroads into the Iranian Islamist leadership, carried out by senior Israelis and Americans who for the most part, particularly on the Israeli side, were not intelligence professionals. From the US standpoint, this was primarily an effort to release US hostages held by Hezbollah in Lebanon and to finance the Contras' campaign in Nicaragua. On the Israeli side, key figures, such as Shimon Peres and Amiram Nir, were convinced that a genuine strategic breakthrough with moderates in the Iranian leadership was in the offing; they were embarrassingly ignorant of the real Iran.[9]

Not all aspects of US involvement in Israel periphery ties were problematic. Uri Lubrani, who as Israeli ambassador in Uganda, Ethiopia, and Iran during the 1960s and 1970s was a major periphery practitioner at the diplomatic level, assesses that for the United States, Israel's periphery links constituted "a positive aspect of our policy. . . . I think this scored us points" in Washington.[10] Ephraim Halevy notes that Israel's marketing of Trident to the United States was minor. "There were other things we marketed much more, such as all our [agricultural and community aid] activity in Africa in the 1960s. That was something the Americans found interesting."[11] The African aid project, essentially an initiative of Foreign Minister Golda Meir, which was cut off abruptly when many African countries severed relations with Israel during the 1973 Yom Kippur War, also received US funding because it was deemed to advance US interests in newly independent African states in ways that Washington could not practice.

An additional and always sensitive aspect of the Israeli–US periphery relationship touches on Muslim perceptions of Jews. As former Mossad head Shabtai Shavit noted, one reason periphery countries welcomed ties to Israel was that "to this day they believe that the keys to the White House are in our pockets."[12] In other words, close clandestine relations with Israel were worthwhile because of Israel's influence in the United States, which was in turn a by-product of US Jewish influence.

Israel did and does indeed have influence in Washington, and it has on occasion undertaken, throughout the original periphery strategy as well as in the current one (see chapter 12), to use that influence in a demonstrable way as a means of strengthening its periphery ties. Turkey, Iran, Ethiopia, and the Iraqi Kurds all requested favors from Israel in Washington and all benefited from these efforts, but Israel has never exercised the kind of influence attributed to it by some of its periphery partners.

As noted in chapter 7, the frequently exaggerated belief in Israel's capacity to influence the United States can in some instances possibly be traced at least in part to latent anti-Semitic beliefs. Yet Israeli representatives rarely if ever protested. Indeed, Mossad operatives generally had few compunctions about exploiting these attitudes toward Jews for Israel's benefit. This was the "protocols [of the elders of Zion]" paradigm at work.

## CONCLUSION

Based on this brief and largely anecdotal discussion, it emerges that the United States, while in some ways and on some occasions a partner to Israel's periphery initiatives, never fully understood them as Israel did—perhaps because as in the case of the Maronites in 1982, it grasped the true dynamic of the relationship as poorly as did Israel, or perhaps, as in the case of Kissinger, Iran, and the Kurds in October 1973, its perceived interests did not correspond with those of Israel—a fact not necessarily fully comprehended at the Israeli end. Then, too, in many cases Israel had little choice but to acquiesce in an imperfect partnership.

The Israeli–US relationship concerning the periphery functioned, like Israel's specific periphery relationships, largely on the basis of interests, not sentiment, and the interests did not always coincide. Currently, Israel is apparently trying to sell Washington some sort of emerging new periphery doctrine (see chapter 13) on the shaky assumption that it corresponds with US interests. In some instances, for example, Ethiopia, this may be the case. In others, particularly ties that constitute a challenge to Turkey's perceived interests, this may not be so.

## NOTES

1. Andrew and Leslie Cockburn, *Dangerous Liaison: The Inside Story of the U.S.–Israeli Covert Relationship*, 1991, p. 100.

2. Declassified US cable traffic published by Amir Oren, *Haaretz*, Sept. 5, 2008 (Hebrew); William Quandt interview, Sept. 10, 2013.

3. Riedel interview.

4. David Kimche and Uri Lubrani interviews.

5. Hart-Davis, *The War That Never Was*.

6. Daniel Kurtzer interview, Europe, July 30, 2010.

7. Samuel Lewis interview, Washington, May 13, 2009.

8. Interview conducted in Israel, May 27, 2011. Identity withheld at request of interviewee.

9. *Becoming Enemies: U.S.–Iran Relations and the Iran–Iraq War, 1979–1988*, pp. 142–43, remarks by Bruce Riedel and Thomas Pickering.

10. Lubrani interview.

11. Halevy interview.
12. Shavit interview. See also chapter 7, note 3: similar remark by Ephraim Halevy.

## Chapter Nine

# End of the First Periphery, 1973–1983

As the periphery doctrine wound down, Israel's regional circumstances began to change radically. We have seen in the course of discussing almost every periphery initiative, from Trident to southern Sudan and from the Kurds to the Maronites, that these operations seemingly had a life of their own that often ended abruptly. All in all, the original periphery doctrine exhausted itself in the period between 1973 and 1983.

There were a number of low points or negative climaxes. During the October 1973 Yom Kippur War, Israel was disappointed when the Iraqi Kurds refused to muster forces that might have obliged Iraq to delay transfer of its divisions to the Golan front. In that same war, Morocco sent a division to bolster Syria and Iraq on the Golan front, and the shah of Iran joined the oil embargo against Israel and the West. In 1975, the shah signed the Algiers treaty with Iraq's Saddam Hussein, cut off Israeli access to Iraqi Kurdistan, and hinted to at least one Arab journalist that he was revising his attitude toward Israel.

By 1979, the shah had been deposed by the Islamic Republic, which immediately became extremely hostile toward Israel, and Ethiopia's Haile Selassie had been toppled by a radical pro-Soviet regime. In 1982–1983, Israel's alliance with the Lebanese Maronites failed abjectly to install a pro-Israel regime in that country and left Israel exposed to years of violence in southern Lebanon.

There was also a positive edge to some of these same developments. In 1977, a peace process began between Israel and Egypt, aided and abetted by Iran and particularly Morocco. Here certainly was one positive outcome of the periphery doctrine: the Israeli leadership availed itself of the good offices of the shah and King Hassan to help bring about a peace process with the most important country of the Arab core, Egypt, thereby seemingly putting an end to conventional Arab–Israel wars. Inevitably, and in some ways happily, peace with Egypt rendered the periphery of far less importance to Israel than it was in the 1950s and 1960s. Today it is significant to note that the Israeli–Egyptian peace has lasted longer than did Trident, which was arguably Israel's most impressive periphery alliance.

Nothing could be more symbolic of the transition from the periphery doctrine to the beginnings of an Arab–Israel peace process than the Camp David meeting of September 5–17, 1978, which brought together US president Jimmy Carter, Egyptian president Anwar Sadat, and Israeli prime minister Menachem Begin. Camp David 1978 produced agreement on the components of Israeli–Egyptian peace. In the midst of that extended conference, the revolutionary dynamic in Iran took a decided turn for the worse. On September 8, "Black Friday," the shah declared martial law and deployed his army to disperse essentially peaceful demonstrations, leading to considerable civilian loss of life. This contributed substantially to the overall snowball effect that brought about the downfall of the Pahlavi dynasty.

In view of the shah's deteriorating situation, I was asked—as de facto chief Mossad analyst on Iran—whether I had any ideas for recruiting international diplomatic support that might prop up his regime. I suggested a joint Israeli–US–Egyptian communiqué from Camp David. Within two days it materialized, its support for the shah tempered by US concern over his human rights abuses so that it sounded as much like a call for nonviolence as a proregime manifesto. It had no effect on events, even if it constituted a then rare instance of public Israeli–Egyptian agreement regarding a strategic development elsewhere in the Middle East.

With the benefit of hindsight, and in view of the opportunities available today to explore the Arab reaction to the periphery approach with a number of Arab strategic thinkers (see chapter 14), the periphery strategy can be seen to have registered both achievements and disappointments in terms of Israel's overall security interests.

Thus, Israel's very capacity to break out of the Arab ring of isolation and form strategic relations on the flanks of the Arab world contributed to its deterrent profile. Of particular note is (the totally unfounded) Egyptian concern lest Israel's strategic presence in Ethiopia and southern Sudan threaten the flow of the Nile waters—Egypt's existential lifeline and a source of near primeval Egyptian strategic fears.

Despite the disappointments of 1973, extremely cost-effective Israeli investments in Kurdistan and South Sudan did tie down hostile Arab forces and signal an Israeli quasi-military presence "behind enemy lines." The operation in Yemen, which "cost" Israel a total of fourteen airdrops of ordnance into Yemeni mountain passes during the mid-1960s—mostly booty from earlier wars with Egypt—constituted a significant contribution toward the demoralization of Egyptian forces in the countdown to the June 1967 Six-Day War, which began with 30,000 Egyptian troops still pinned down in Yemen.

There were economic benefits, too, particularly oil deals with Iran and Oman. And the CIA duly noted Israel's periphery successes, thereby enhancing the Israeli–US strategic relationship.

On the other hand, the intelligence gleaned from alliances such as Trident was never of consistent high quality: the relationship's value was little more than the fact of its very existence. Certainly Trident was never a serious alliance of, say, NATO caliber. The shah's 1975 justification for his ties with Israel, which boiled down to "your enemy's enemy is your friend," at best describes a temporary alliance of convenience. As with Morocco and even the Kurds, Israeli officials were aware at the height of Trident's success, too, that the Iranians and the Turks had read "the Protocols [of the Elders of Zion]," meaning a portion of their adherence to the alliance with Israel derived from the exaggerated belief of periphery partners that Israel, through the US Jewish lobby, could petition Washington successfully on their behalf whenever the need arose. This was hardly the basis for a healthy and stable relationship.

The fiasco with the Lebanese Maronites was so traumatic for the Israeli security community, which felt betrayed by Maronite abandonment of pledges of partnership against Syria and the Palestine Liberation Organization, that it has avoided such relationships with minorities ever since. In Israel's eyes, few could outdo the Maronites for cynical exploitation of its goodwill in 1982–1983.

Certainly it is fair to assess that Israel's periphery alliances were based to a large extent on self-interest—even cynical self-interest—on the part of all sides. That, of course, is the norm in many international ties, but it was particularly problematic when it was the only type of relationship Israel had with any of its neighbors.

The sole exceptions were some of the links with minorities, where Israel's support reflected a genuine degree of both sympathy for and empathy with those suffering at Arab hands. For their part, the southern Sudanese and the Kurds, both now independent or quasi-independent, profess genuine gratitude for Israeli help tendered decades ago. Perhaps this was because Israel's clandestine backing included not only military support but extensive civilian medical aid as well as meetings with a charismatic and genuinely caring Israeli leader such as Prime Minister Golda Meir. Whether these were assets that Israel could "take to the bank" strategically is another question. Moreover, as noted regarding the Maronites, not all minorities that Israel aided responded this way.

A more comprehensive assessment of the strategic efficacy of the periphery doctrine will be attempted in our concluding chapter, when the evidence of a new ring of hostility and the possible emergence of a new periphery are before us. Meanwhile, the next few chapters will examine the events and dynamics of some three decades of Arab–Israel interaction that separate the two peripheries, with specific attention to the issues of "periphery nostalgia," Israeli skepticism, and a collation of Arab strategic assessments regarding the doctrine.

*II*

# Ramifications

# Chapter Ten

# Iran

## Periphery Nostalgia and Its Costs

Israel's close strategic alliance with Iran ended in 1979 with the fall of the shah and the creation of the Islamic Republic. This chapter looks at the inclination since 1979 on the part of significant Israeli policy makers to view the Islamic Republic and its prolonged hostility toward Israel as a temporary phenomenon, not representative of the true Iran and its interests, and accordingly, to argue that the Tehran regime can be bought off or undermined by Israel through subterfuge, propaganda, arms sales, and any other means available.

We argue that to the contrary, since 1979 there has been no objective basis for assessing that the regime in Tehran is fragile and can easily be toppled, that it can be persuaded to reconcile with Israel, or that if the regime does fall, it will be replaced by an alternative establishment that is friendly to Israel. While the Islamic Republic displays numerous intolerant and violent tendencies that have produced many dissidents, it has survived a prolonged war with Iraq during the 1980s and more recently, heavy international sanctions. Judging by Iranian elections, the majority of Iranians appear to support at least the idea of the regime, which has struck deep institutional and cultural roots. Predictions of the regime's imminent demise appear to be expressions of wishful thinking, inspired largely by well-meaning dissidents and in the case of Israel, by periphery nostalgia derived from ignorance.

Periphery nostalgia is the presumption that because Iran has historic tensions with the Arab world and because one Iranian regime, that of the shah, seemingly aligned itself strategically with Israel over the course of two decades, this pattern of alliance and shared strategic interests must through some form of historical determination or strategic norm, continue to manifest itself in Israel's relations with Iran. The periphery nostalgia approach toward Iran has caused Israel repeated damage at the strategic level.

Dan Eldar, a former senior Mossad analyst, explains that this phenomenon has not been confined to Israel:

> Intelligence and academic experts outside of Iran adjusted slowly to the change that took place there. For many years their thinking and analysis failed due to the shock of surprise and helpless anger over their failure [to anticipate the revolution] and due to intellectual and mental difficulties in "digesting" the Islamic revolution. These failings found expression . . . in a strong desire, sometimes conscious and sometimes not, to turn back the wheel of history. The hope to quickly restore the Shah's regime resonated negatively on the intelligence assessment regarding Khomeini's Iran. Intelligence consumers/ decision-makers sought in the early days of the Islamic Republic an assessment that would limit its days and announce the first glimmer of the near return of the Shah's regime. [1]

Evidently, a few Israeli policy makers still have not been weaned from this syndrome. True, for the most part periphery nostalgia toward Iran has characterized the approach of a minority of Israeli strategic policy makers, but on occasion, as in the 1985 Iran–Contra affair, this minority was able to channel Israeli policy even when many senior Israeli security officials expressed skepticism or outright opposition. In recent years, the nostalgia phenomenon has taken the form not of outreach to Iran as in the 1980s but rather of confident predictions regarding the impending downfall of the Tehran regime if it is simply attacked or its population saturated with the appropriate propaganda.

Note the evolution of the approach—from seeking reconciliation to seeking regime change: from searching for moderate Iranians who can exercise influence within the Tehran regime during the 1980s to the current argument that moderate Iranians are poised to take back the reins of power in Tehran or that Iranian minorities, such as the Azeris, will revolt if the regime is just given a strong enough push. This approach in turn has nurtured the development of Israel's relationship with Azerbaijan, which borders Iran to its north, where a large Iranian Azeri minority lives.

In recent years Israel has confined itself in its confrontation with the regime to the use of limited means for inhibiting Iran's nuclear program. It has not engaged in all-out war and has not spent hundreds of millions of dollars on satellite propaganda broadcasts, as some have suggested, but the strategic significance of periphery nostalgia in the present context cannot be dismissed out of hand. In the 1980s, it caused Israel to make foolish decisions that damaged its relations with the United States and Egypt. In August 2012, a serving minister of defense responsible for decision making regarding Israel's response to Iran's nuclear program publicly expressed confidence—with no basis in objective analysis—that a successful Israeli attack on Iran would give Israel sufficient breathing space for a few years until a friendly regime takes over in Tehran. In view of statements like these, no one can argue that periphery nostalgia is not liable to dangerously affect Israeli strategic decision making.

Here, by way of comparison, and before entering into detail regarding Iran, a brief word is in order regarding Turkey, the third partner in Trident. Israel's strategic relations with Turkey over more than half a century have been generally more stable than relations with Iran, but also shallower: during this period there was no Kurdish cause, no energy issues, and no extensive arms deals keeping the two countries together as was the case with Israel and Iran. Accordingly, the radical downswing in Israeli–Turkish relations since the advent to power of Prime Minister Recep Tayyip Erdoğan and his Islamist party has generated far less nostalgia than did the Iran case. True, in recent years one can detect a kind of resentment or "wounded" attitude in Israel as it confronts the extraordinary and provocative Middle East regional outreach—without Israel—developed by Turkey under a moderate Islamist regime. True, some Israelis with extensive knowledge of Turkey have tried to argue that Erdoğan does not represent the "real" Turkey, but no one in Israel is suggesting alternatives to working with a pragmatic Islamic regime.

Indeed, repeated democratic elections in Turkey have verified Erdoğan's credentials. Moreover, Erdoğan never fully cut relations: Israeli–Turkish commerce thrived and grew even at the lowest point in relations after the 2010 Mavi Marmara incident. And after the March 2013 Netanyahu apology over that incident there were hopes that some sort of strategic relationship could be repaired, though Turkish support for Hamas in the July 2014 Gaza war constituted yet another setback. Moreover, as we shall see in chapter 13, Israel wasted no time crying over spilled milk and hastened after the Mavi Marmara incident to develop relations with a new periphery of countries bordering on Turkey by land and sea—albeit a periphery that unlike the case of Azerbaijan and Iran, is not intended in any way to threaten Turkey but merely to contain it.

## IRAN NOSTALGIA IN THE 1980s: IRAN–CONTRA AND BEYOND

Shortly after the Islamic revolution of 1979, Iran found itself at war with Iraq—a highly destructive war that lasted eight years. In terms of its strategic interests, the most obvious position for Israel to adopt toward this war was to ensure that neither Iran nor Iraq emerged from it significantly stronger— indeed, that both emerged weaker. Postrevolutionary Iran had displayed absolutely no warmth toward Israel and constantly called for its destruction. Tehran also argued that Israel owed Iran hundreds of millions of dollars in payments for oil deals carried out during the shah's reign (we recall that Israelis with business interests in Iran had been guided by the government in Jerusalem during the shah's final months in power to ensure that at any given time, they owed Iran money and not the reverse). Iraq under Saddam Hussein presented an equally distasteful and hostile regime that had participated in every Arab war against Israel.

Throughout the war's eight years, Israel, often in consultation with the United States, made tactical decisions regarding arms supplies and other war-related issues as the need arose. Israel, like other countries, has never been a saint when the issue at stake is making money from arms sales and ensuring a cash flow for Israel's own research and development efforts regarding weaponry. Nor did Israel tilt only toward Iran during the 1980s: when Jordan's Red Sea port of Aqaba, adjacent to Eilat, became a primary supply channel for Iraq because the latter's Persian Gulf outlets were blocked by Iran, Israel did not make a fuss.

But arms supply to Iran represented more than just pragmatism and business. As Yitzhak Hofi, head of the Mossad from the mid-1970s to the early 1980s, relates: "After the fall of the shah in 1979 and the rise to power of Iranian fundamentalism, all kinds of attempts were made and all kinds of episodes aimed at links with Iran took place, some not pleasant. When I headed the Mossad, we tried with all our power to continue to maintain contact with the Iranians, against the advice of the Americans. Thus for example we supplied retread tires for their [F-4] Phantoms"[2] in the early stages of the Iran–Iraq War.

In 1985, Iran's weapons needs and Israel's near compulsive need to exploit them embroiled Israel in a major international scandal: the Iran–Contra affair. The protagonists were an Iranian swindler named Manucher Ghorbanifar, a clique of extreme right wingers in the Reagan administration, and a group of Israelis—some greedy, some abysmally misinformed—who convinced themselves that Israeli weapons supply to Iran could bring about a major turning point in Iran's attitude toward Israel. The affair involved the indirect provision of arms by Reagan administration officials to the anti-Sandinista Contra rebels in Nicaragua, based on money received for supplying US-made Hawk surface-to-air missiles and TOW antitank missiles to Iran. Israel supplied the arms to Iran and turned over the profits to the United States in return for replacement arms. The Reagan administration officials bypassed the US prohibition of arms supply to the Contras and to Iran by using funds generated through Israel's sale of the arms to Iran to aid the Contras. As part of this convoluted deal, the Iranians undertook to secure the freedom of US hostages held by Hezbollah in Lebanon; indeed, some were released.

Israel's reward—beyond the close collaboration with the United States— was projected to be in the form of a thaw in relations with Iran. Israel also hoped to strengthen the Iranian war effort against Iraq, which was perceived (particularly after Israel's destruction in 1981 of the Osirak nuclear reactor near Baghdad) as by far the more significant military threat.

The initial US instigator of Iran–Contra was Michael Ledeen, a former CIA official and advocate of regime change in Iran from then to this day. He discussed it with Prime Minister Shimon Peres in 1985. A Saudi arms dealer and power broker, Adnan Khashoggi, was also involved. In the course of nearly two years of contacts, the project evolved from one ostensibly involving antiregime elements to contacts with presumed regime moderates.

The initial Israeli protagonists of Iran–Contra were Yaakov Nimrodi, formerly Israel's military attaché in Tehran and now a businessman with lingering commercial ties in Iran, and Al Schwimmer, a businessman who had founded Israel's aircraft industry. They were backed by Prime Minister Shimon Peres. In a second phase of the dealings, Peres appointed Amiram Nir, an ambitious former journalist and now his counterterrorism adviser, to lead a secret mission to Tehran that ended in fiasco. It was around this time that David Kimche, former deputy head of the Mossad and now director-general of the foreign ministry, was added to the Israeli team.

All the Israelis involved believed that one way or another, a moderate faction involved in a power struggle in Iran would be strengthened through the arms supply, thereby paving the way to a strategic breakthrough in Israeli–Iranian relations. At the time, Israel had few intelligence sources inside Iran, and it was hoped the new contacts would prove useful in this connection. Concern to ensure the safety of Iran's Jewish community was also cited as a factor; in its early days, the Islamic Republic had executed a leader of that community on trumped-up charges, and it was preventing the orderly exit to Israel or elsewhere of the remaining Jews—a sensitive issue for all Israelis.

The entire Israeli clique that pushed through the deal ignored the doubts and admonitions of Israel's own intelligence establishment. Most of its principals had already plotted in 1982 to remove Ayatollah Khomeini. Now they were persuaded to work with the Iranian leadership. The Israelis were dealing with Iranians of doubtful influence, who had a reputation for shady deals. Because lines of contact and command were problematic and at times amateurish, the Hawk missiles that were delivered turned out to be an obsolete model, and the TOW delivery was canceled by Iran. Needless to say, there was no strategic breakthrough in relations with Iran.

The affair was revealed to the public when uninvolved Iranian officials who had discovered the source of the weaponry leaked it to the Lebanese press in late 1986. A major scandal ensued in the United States, involving court cases, resignations, and dismissals. In Israel, where no laws had been broken, the commotion was more subdued.[3]

There was damage to both Israeli–US and Israeli–Egyptian relations. In Washington, Israel's credibility, and particularly the credibility of its intelligence establishment, was hurt. As described by Bruce Riedel, then a senior CIA official and in ensuing years Middle East adviser to President Clinton, the Israelis were so desperate to restore their relationship with Iran "that they were willing to enlist a crew of liars and no-goods to help with the rapprochement. Any remotely objective review of the evidence would have revealed to them that these people were not going to deliver. . . . What's very odd about this, of course, is that it's at this very moment that Iranians are building Hezbollah and cleaning the Israelis' clock in Lebanon."

Riedel acknowledges that a number of senior US officials, such as Robert McFarlane and Zbigniew Brzezinski, shared the Israelis' belief that they confronted an opportunity to deal with a moderate faction in Iran. But "it is the Israelis who are pitching this possibility of a strategic dialogue. And among the people who are pitching it, the key figure is Shimon Peres."[4] "The most enthusiastic nostalgia arguer [concerning Iran] was Shimon Peres."[5] (Other senior US diplomats of that period point to Ariel Sharon as the key figure in initiating the Israeli–Iranian arms relationship in the early 1980s and to Yitzhak Rabin, minister of defense in 1985, as being the prime mover in efforts to recruit US support for an Israeli–Iranian rapprochement in 1985.[6] This appears doubtful, insofar as all the Israeli principals were connected to Peres, not to Rabin. Moreover, in Israel Rabin was understood to be very cautious regarding Iran–Contra.[7])

Meanwhile Egypt, which had signed a historic peace treaty with Israel barely a few years before Iran–Contra, saw that operation as an Israeli betrayal of Jerusalem's true interest in developing closer relations with the mainstream Arab world. Cairo was still harboring resentment over the First Lebanon War of 1982–1983, in which Israel collaborated with the Lebanese Maronites, another periphery partner, in an abortive and destructive attempt to render the Lebanese power structure friendlier to Jerusalem. By late 1987, scarcely a year after Iran–Contra was revealed to the world, both Peres and Rabin went out of their way to assure Egypt's Mustafa Khalil, a former prime minister and their guest in Jerusalem, that "there is not a single Israeli that I am aware of who could compromise with Khomeini" [Peres] and that Israel was not supplying "a single nut or bolt" to Iran [Rabin].[8] Khalil had warned Israel not to support Iran, which was hindering Egypt's peace efforts and supporting Islamic fundamentalism in the region. Both Khalil and the Peres–Rabin team were presumably aware of persistent press allegations at the time that Israel was continuing to supply arms to Iran even after the Iran–Contra fiasco.[9]

In short, in the eyes of most of Washington and the moderate Middle East countries as well as many knowledgeable Israelis, Israel had aligned itself with the wrong camp. Major General Shlomo Gazit, a retired head of IDF intelligence who was asked by Peres early in the Iran–Contra affair to supervise the activities of Nimrodi and Schwimmer, stepped aside after ascertaining that the two were involved mainly to make money from the arms sales and after meeting with Ghorbanifar and ascertaining that he was a swindler. "The idea of a breakthrough with Iran was legitimate and worth examining," Gazit concludes, but the substance was lacking. [10] In the assessment of Gideon Rafael, a veteran Israeli diplomat, "To believe that the victory of Khomeinism will lead to its overthrow by a junta of generals, bound to Israel by gratitude is, to say the least, a sign of political infantilism." [11] Riedel concludes with advice about Israel for US decision makers, "We should be careful to weigh even close allies' advice." [12]

## CONTEMPORARY ISRAELI "NOSTALGIA" ATTITUDES TOWARD IRAN

As noted earlier, no one in Israel seems to be advocating today that Israel link up with and strengthen a moderate camp in Iran—whether by fomenting a coup or supplying arms. Yet there is a strong lobby of Israeli security thinkers who have convinced themselves that Iranian moderates can and will take power if Israel and/or the United States just gives the Tehran regime a push. In other words, this is an Israeli regime-change school of thought. As with Iran–Contra, its dual assessment that the ayatollahs' regime is teetering and that when it falls, it will be replaced by moderates rather than some less friendly faction, appears to have no basis in objective analysis of Iran's politics and power structure.

Here, in chronological order, are a few overt examples of this approach, most from the past decade:

- A US Middle East expert relates: "In late 1997, Netanyahu sent his chief adviser on Iran to Washington carrying the message that the election of Khatami as president represented an 'irreversible' trend toward moderation in Iranian politics, which should be encouraged. The following summer, 1998 . . . at a breakfast with Zalman Shoval, Israel's ambassador to the United States, [he] told us that 'Israel is not the enemy of Iran.'" [13]
- Uri Lubrani, former Israeli ambassador in Tehran and for years a key figure influencing Israel Ministry of Defense thinking about Iran and Lebanon, relates that during the countdown to the US invasion of Iraq in 2003, "I spoke with Paul Wolfowitz and Doug Feith [both senior Pentagon officials] and others and told them 'go for Iran.' . . . At that time I believed that [regime change in Tehran] could be achieved without moving a single American soldier, just with money. . . . Any new regime in Iran . . . will

look for a way to the United States and one of those ways will be through us."[14]

- According to an official US document cited in the Israeli press, then Mossad head Meir Dagan proposed to the United States in the summer of 2007 that "Israel and the United States can replace the regime in Iran. . . . [W]e can bring them to postpone the nuclear project."[15]

- Minister of Defense Ehud Barak (described in an interview as "the decision-maker") in August 2012: "[T]he real story is the contest between Iran's nuclearization and the fall of the current regime of the ayatollahs in Iran. If we succeed in pushing off the nuclear program by six or eight or 10 years, there's a good chance that the regime will not survive until the critical moment."[16]

- Former Deputy Minister of Defense Ephraim Sneh, commenting prior to Iran's June 2013 elections: "The weeks remaining until the elections are an opportunity to bring about a revolutionary change from within, by the Iranian people themselves. For this we need a dramatic acceleration of the sanctions and the dispatch of a clear message of support and allegiance to the Iranian people."[17]

- In November 2013, a group of thirteen recently retired US generals and admirals reported hearing from senior Israeli national security experts during a visit to Israel that should the United States "ratchet up" sanctions, the younger Iranian population could sweep the regime from power, and "a delay to the nuclear program lasting three to five years . . . may provide a sufficient window to allow this to occur."[18]

Occasionally in the course of recent years, Israelis have apparently traveled to Iran on humanitarian-type missions. For example, in the spring of 2006 Israeli development experts were reportedly allowed into Iran using non-Israeli travel documents to assess the damage done by an earthquake to infrastructure that they had built with Israeli expertise in the shah's day.[19] Such gestures and, indeed, signals to Iran that Israel bears it no ill will and looks forward to the day when relations can be renewed, are not the issue at stake in our discussion of periphery nostalgia toward Iran. Nor is the inclination of Israelis and Iranians, on the rare occasions when they do find themselves in the same venue at a scientific or strategic conference, to seek one another out. I recall such a meeting held in Amman, Jordan, in the mid-1990s, attended by many Arabs and a few Israelis and Iranians. At breaks for meals, the Israelis and Iranians gravitated to the same table while the Arabs looked on, mystified.

Nor, for that matter, is the issue the election in Iran of a president supported by reformists: Khatami in the period 1997–2005 and Rouhani in 2013. With all due respect to these leaders, in Iran real authority is held by the supreme leader and the religious establishment that designed the Islamic

Republic as a theocratic dictatorship and by the Revolutionary Guards, which maintain a near monopoly on coercive power.

Rather, the question is: What made senior Israeli strategists believe in the 1980s that Iran's "good guys" were simply waiting for Israel to reach out, and what makes them believe today that with a little help, the Islamic Republic will fall and genuine moderates will rise to power? A number of factors appear to be at work.

One is cited by former Mossad head Ephraim Halevy: "We think we can be king-makers" in the Middle East: with the Palestinians, with Lebanon in 1982, and with the Iranians. "This is nonsense."[20]

A second and more pervasive factor involves a drastic misunderstanding of what Israel's state-to-state periphery relationships were really about in the 1960s and 1970s. There is an inclination among many Israelis who recall those days to glorify them as a genuine meeting of hearts and minds between like-minded Middle Eastern peoples who are natural allies. As we saw in chapter 2, from the standpoint of both Turkey and Iran this was not the case: there is persuasive evidence that the shah himself saw his relationship with Israel—the only relationship Israel has ever had with Iran in modern times— in a manipulative and cynical mold.

It follows from this historical misperception that these same Israelis will-fully or erroneously engage in wishful thinking and ignore the dramatic change that has taken place in Iran's power structure since the shah's day. Most Iranians accept the framework of the Islamic Republic, with its highly guided democracy. If Iran is attacked, they are more likely to rally round the regime than seek to change it. If anything does bring down the Iranian regime it won't be outside forces but rather, as in the case of the Soviet Union, internal processes largely unaffected by the machinations of external regime changers and in accordance with a timetable independent of their activities. Moreover, if the regime does for some reason fall, it is more likely to be replaced by an Islamic military regime drawn from the all-powerful Revolutionary Guards than by a liberal minority that in some ways harks all the way back to the Bakhtiars, the Sanjabis, and the Bazargans, who made a hash of attempting secular rule in early 1979 (see chapter 2).

Here, then, is the real danger of periphery nostalgia: that Israel will act on these faulty conceptions, that it will risk its credibility with its friends by advising them to act on these same mistaken assessments, and that it will consciously or inadvertently ignore prospects for coexistence with its immediate Arab neighbors because it convinces itself of the seeming immutability of its periphery relationships.

# NOTES

1. Dan Eldar, "Countries in crisis: the border between a useful intelligence assessment and a superfluous prophecy," *Mabat Malam* 68, Mar. 2014 (Hebrew).

2. Yitzhak Hofi interview, *Yedion Malam*, no. 23, Feb. 2000 (Hebrew).

3. Iran–Contra is described in detail in Yossi Melman and Dan Raviv, *The Imperfect Spies: The History of Israeli Intelligence*, 1989, Sidgwick & Jackson. Shlomo Gazit added important details: e-mail correspondence, Aug. 4, 2013.

4. Multiple authors, *Becoming Enemies: U.S.–Iran Relations and the Iran–Iraq War, 1979–1988*, pp. 90–91, 128–29, 142–43.

5. Bruce Riedel interview.

6. Regarding Sharon, interview with retired senior US diplomat, May 27, 2011; regarding Rabin, Thomas Pickering in *Becoming Enemies*, p. 143.

7. Interview with Shlomo Gazit, June 15, 2013.

8. "Peres Pledges No Compromise with Khomeyni," *Jerusalem Post*, Nov. 18, 1987, FBIS-NES-87-223.

9. See Rowland Evans and Robert Novak, "Is Israel Selling Arms to Iran Again?" *Washington Post*, Sept. 9, 1987.

10. Interview with Shlomo Gazit.

11. Gideon Rafael, "Israel and the Iran 'affair': The danger of underhand dealings," *Jerusalem Post*, Nov. 21, 1986.

12. Bruce Riedel, "Has US forgotten lessons of its first war with Iran?" *Al-Monitor*, Apr. 11, 2012.

13. Thomas W. Lippman, Middle East Institute, Washington, e-mail correspondence, Jan. 4, 2013. See also Steve Rodan, "Iran, Israel reportedly forging contacts," *Jerusalem Post*, Sept. 9, 1997.

14. Uri Lubrani interview, Tel Aviv, July 27, 2009.

15. Aluf Benn, "Dagan and the mission impossible," *Haaretz*, Dec. 8, 2010, citing US cables leaked by Wikileaks.

16. Ari Shavit interview with "The Decision Maker," *Haaretz*, Aug. 10, 2012.

17. Efraim Sneh, "The option under the table," *Yedioth Ahronoth*, May 30, 2013.

18. Walter Pincus, *Washington Post*, Nov. 28, 2013.

19. Meir Javedanfar, "Was Ariel Sharon Israel's Secret Channel to Iran?" *Al-Monitor*, Apr. 22, 2013.

20. Ephraim Halevy interview.

# Chapter Eleven

# Israeli Skeptics

Between the mid-1950s and the early 1980s, a fairly large circle of Israelis linked to national security issues became familiar with one aspect or another of periphery operations. Yet few had a broad and deep enough appreciation of the doctrine as a grand strategy to be able to pass judgment on its relative success or failure or, indeed, to be interested in doing so. Nor, apparently, was the doctrine itself the subject of any sort of thorough and periodic evaluation process in national security circles. Moreover, the almost entirely clandestine nature of the periphery doctrine reduced the likelihood that academic circles would scrutinize and review it. Ben Gurion's diaries, for example, contain passages on initiatives toward Iran and Turkey dating to 1957–1958 that remained blotted out by the authorities through pure inertia until in 2012 this author requested their release to the public.

The absence of objective outsiders who had sufficient knowledge of the grand strategy in action to pass judgment on it was an inevitable by-product of secrecy. The problem afflicts virtually all clandestine services. The doctrine was implemented primarily by the Mossad, by means of covert activity. The foreign and defense ministries were aware of periphery activities and operations on a need-to-know basis. Thus, Israel's ambassadors in Iran, Turkey, and Ethiopia were kept in the general picture and in some cases, when the ambassador himself had a strong regional background and cultivated very high-level ties, could be considered protagonists of the policy themselves. Defense ministry and IDF personnel were introduced to specific operations where their expertise was required, as in Yemen, South Sudan, and Kurdistan, and where military assistance was tendered in conjunction with the Mossad. Israeli military attachés in Iran, Turkey, and Ethiopia were local accomplices but also coordinated military aid and liaison directly and separately from the Mossad/periphery connection. Occasionally, expertise was recruited from the "Shin Bet" (General Security Service) and from a variety of ministries, depending on the issue area involved.

## WHO WERE THE SKEPTICS?

This backdrop renders the views of a few known skeptics all the more interesting from a historical standpoint and all the more relevant for the future, and indeed, there were skeptics. They can be broken down into two categories. One group consisted of academics and related Arab affairs experts who enjoyed access to security knowledge as consultants or who served as occasional diplomats. They took exception to the periphery concept at the conceptual level, judging the extent to which in their view, it became a zero-sum game played out at the expense of Israel's potential for establishing peaceful relations with its Arab neighbors.

The second, consisting mainly of military intelligence practitioners and commanders, confined its critique to the pragmatic level. Either the doctrine simply didn't produce enough positive results to justify the effort invested, or it created exaggerated expectations regarding alliance-type behavior that inevitably left Israel disappointed and conceivably even less prepared for conflict.

For this second group, the behavior of the Kurds, Iran, and Morocco during the 1973 Yom Kippur War is a primary case in point. Kurdish leader Mulla Mustafa Barzani bowed to Iranian and US pressure and ignored his prior commitment to Israel to mobilize and maneuver his troops to pin down Iraqi divisions that might otherwise reach Israel's Syria front as an expeditionary force. The shah of Iran joined the oil embargo, and Moroccan forces were sent to the Syria front as early as February 1973 and then reinforced in September, seeing brief action against Israel in October.

Professor Shimon Shamir of Tel Aviv University, a former Israeli ambassador to Cairo and to Amman, personifies the first group, the conceptual skeptics. His views are worthy of an extended presentation.[1] "This is not the conceptual framework in which I think," Shamir begins. He is an "Arabist," an expert on Arab society and a fluent Arabic speaker. His intellectual and professional orientation is toward studying and coexisting with Israel's neighbors, the surrounding Arab world—not the non-Arab periphery, in which he has little faith.

> We made peace with Egypt, with Jordan, we could have made peace with Syria. . . . These are the lands of the core, their importance lies in their borders with us. In contrast, the [lands of the] periphery fell by the wayside, one by one, beginning with Iran. . . . [The periphery approach] in fact means that we abandon our main front, on which our future existence depends, the Arab Islamic world, and link up with its enemies. After all, the Kurdish connection

is against the regime in Iraq, against Arabism, the Lebanese minorities were against Syrian Arabism. . . . This reflected an element of despair. . . . Our linking up with non-Arab actors in the Middle East just exacerbated the [Arab] hatred. . . . My informed opinion is that all our activity in the non-Arab sphere was understood as subversion and as proof of our country's historical mission [to destabilize the Arab world on behalf of imperialism]. . . . We joined the enemies of Arabism.

Shamir draws a sharp distinction between Israel's periphery links with Morocco and Oman—Sunni Arab states—and with non-Arabs, such as Iran, Turkey, and the Kurds: "These are not two expressions of the same strategy, these are opposites," perhaps not in the eyes of those who maintained Israel's links with Morocco and the Kurds within the same bureaucratic framework but in Arab eyes, according to Shamir. Here he distinguishes between Morocco's success in maintaining a long-term clandestine relationship with Israel and the failure of another Maghreb Arab leader, Habib Bourguiba of Tunisia, to initiate a peace process in the 1960s. "The Moroccans played it very cleverly. When Bourguiba tried, he was [branded] a traitor. . . . The Moroccans always knew how to balance and do things with agreement and coordination, meaning when they chaperoned the Dayan–Tohami talks [in 1977, leading up to Anwar Sadat's breakthrough visit to Jerusalem]."

Shamir views Israel's links with Middle Eastern minorities as again, a separate category, but one as problematic as links with the region's non-Arab states. "Whenever a minority was prepared to cooperate with us this was both pragmatic and temporary. . . . They knew that ultimately their future was linked with the Arab world within which they lived. . . . They can't rely on Israeli bayonets all the time."

Referring to instances such as Israel's attempt to sell the shah of Iran sophisticated weapons technology on the eve of the Iranian revolution (see chapter 2, "The Northern Triangle"), Shamir concludes: "Frequently [Israeli periphery practitioners] understood the immediate benefit of ties but not their limited horizons."

Shamir identifies himself with Sharett's school of diplomacy, which in Israel's early years went to great lengths to explore possible peace breakthroughs with Nasser's Egypt and other Arab interlocutors, in many cases with US mediation, but in some instances by means of direct, secret contacts. These initiatives are the stuff of extensive historical narratives and analysis that have filled volumes. All the initiatives failed until the 1977 Dayan–Tohami contacts in Morocco, which produced the Sadat trip to Jerusalem, the 1978 Camp David accords, and the 1979 Israeli–Egyptian peace treaty. Sharett and many others believed that Israel missed more than one prior opportunity to make peace with Egypt and that in some cases, for example, IDF reprisal raids into the Gaza Strip and the Jordanian West Bank in 1955–1956, it actually sabotaged chances for a breakthrough.

The Labor party mainstream, which ruled Israel throughout most of this period, believed otherwise. Whether the prime minister was David Ben Gurion, Levi Eshkol, or Golda Meir, he or she was consistently skeptical and suspicious of these initiatives and generally believed that Arab nationalism under Nasser's leadership was far too hostile and that only a militarily powerful Israel could eventually talk peace with the Arabs on a level playing field.

Our discussion of the periphery doctrine in action does not seek to settle this controversy or, indeed, even to enter into it. The question our inquiry asks in connection with peace initiatives is whether the periphery was an obstacle to peace. The answer it arrives at is a resounding negative: if anything, the periphery facilitated contacts with the Arabs and contributed incentives for the Arabs to make peace by painting Israel as a strong and resourceful country that could not be dealt with by any other means.

Sharett, incidentally, cannot be listed as a periphery skeptic if only because his governmental service in Israeli public life ended in 1956, before Trident was created and the periphery doctrine took form. Sharett did have extensive knowledge of Levant minorities, going back to his tenure as head of the Jewish Agency's Political Department during the 1930s. And he was skeptical about links with at least some of them, particularly the Maronites, as demonstrated in his 1954 correspondence with Ben Gurion, who enthusiastically championed the idea of an Israeli-backed Christian buffer state to Israel's north (see chapter 5, "The Levant Minorities"). Both Shimon Shamir and Sharett's son Yaakov, who administers Sharett's archive, believe that Sharett would have opposed the periphery doctrine had he remained in public office. Yaakov Sharett remains convinced to this day that the periphery doctrine is an exaggerated concept that was "a consequence of the feverish imagination of various interested parties."[2]

Additional skeptical assessments of the doctrine are of a much more pragmatic nature. Abba Eban wrote at one point to Ben Gurion, pointing out that Israel had little in common with its new Trident partners, Iran and Turkey, and that military alliances among small states were of little value in the nuclear age since all ultimately relied on the superpowers, the United States and the Soviet Union.[3] Certainly the events that took place between 1973 and 1983 produced skeptics and cautionary advisers at the operational level. The problematic response of the Kurds, the shah of Iran, and the king of Morocco to Israel's quandary in the early days of the Yom Kippur War has already been noted. Referring to the Yom Kippur War, former Mossad head Ephraim Halevy agrees that "when there were testing points, the periphery did not pass the test."[4]

Yet Israel's disappointment did not keep it from maintaining its ties with these same actors after the war. In the case of the shah, as we have seen, his decision in March 1975 to close Iraqi Kurdistan to Israeli access, along with additional warning signs, did not in any way cool Israel's ardor or, for that matter, reduce the scope of Trident ties. Only the 1982–1983 fiasco in Lebanon with the Maronites very clearly did negatively affect Israel's readiness to explore contacts with additional non-Arab or non-Muslim minorities.

Thus it transpired that within the security establishment, these events generated little by way of skeptical—or for that matter any other—conceptual analysis as to whether the periphery doctrine was a smart investment. One apparent exception was Yehoshafat Harkabi, who was head of IDF intelligence in the mid-1950s and a strategic adviser to Prime Minister Yitzhak Rabin and Defense Minister Shimon Peres in the mid-1970s. Harkabi, known to one and all as "Fati," also had an illustrious academic career at the Hebrew University as a professor specializing in Arab and particularly Palestinian studies.

Harkabi's career path in some ways paralleled that of Yuval Ne'eman, who was his deputy in IDF intelligence in the mid-1950s, served as a science adviser to Peres in the mid-1970s, and developed an academic career as a nuclear scientist before turning to right-wing politics. According to Dr. Matti Steinberg, an academic expert on the Palestinians who was closely associated with Harkabi for many years, Ne'eman and Harkabi engaged in an extensive off-and-on argument about the periphery policy: Ne'eman was an ardent supporter and Harkabi, an opponent. In 1975, when both men were working for Peres, Harkabi wrote a brief analysis, "Lessons from the Kurdish affair" (which the author was unable to locate), explaining that the doctrine had failed for lack of periphery partners on which Israel could truly depend. [5]

During the 1970s, 1980s, and 1990s, Harkabi published a number of important analyses of the Israel–Arab conflict and related strategic issues. None of these analyses bothers even to mention the periphery doctrine as a strategy by which Israel responded to the Arab threat or in any other context. Similarly, Aharon Yariv, another former head of military intelligence, who in the course of an academic career heading the Jaffee Center for Strategic Studies from 1977 to 1993, lectured and wrote extensively on Israel's strategic requirements, once noted that "the concept of periphery is very deeply imbedded in the minds" of Israel's national security policy makers[6] and according to one former senior officer who asked his opinion, believed the doctrine had failed.[7] On the other hand, he endorsed Israel's airdrop operation in Yemen during the early 1960s, operation *rotev* (see chapter 4, "The Southern Periphery"), as a profitable investment both operationally and in intelligence terms.[8] In 1987 he advocated that Israel support Iraq against Iran in the two countries' prolonged war, calling for a "more balanced view" but acknowledging that he represented a minority among Israeli strategic thinkers.[9] (Here it bears mention that by 1987, several years after the effective collapse of the periphery, many voices were heard in Israel warning against an ongoing tilt toward Iran in the context of the Iran–Iraq War, and the

United States was pressuring Israel heavily to desist. See chapter 10, "Iran: Periphery Nostalgia and Its Costs.")

Evidently neither Harkabi nor Yariv were disciples of Sharett: neither apparently believed Israel had missed peace opportunities by virtue of its commitment to periphery links. To the extent we can reconstruct their skeptical approach, they simply felt that a cost–benefit analysis would in some cases find the periphery approach wanting. This point of view was perhaps best summed up by Alouph Hareven, who was intimately involved in the Mossad's initial Kurdistan and southern Sudan operations. In an apparent response to the Harkabi critique of 1975, Hareven wrote in 1980: "There were those who did a precise accounting of profit and loss, who never stopped asking questions like: What are Israel's practical objectives? What did Israel achieve at the diplomatic level? The strategic level? [Some argue that Israel's] pressure in Kurdistan had no influence on the course of history."[10]

## ASSESSING THE SKEPTICS' POINT OF VIEW

One possible reason behind the skeptics' negative view of the periphery doctrine is that they held a relatively narrow perception of the substance of the periphery and due to either lack of knowledge or a minimalist conceptual view, confined their criticism to the performance of a select few of the better-known periphery partners and operations: Iran and Turkey (Trident), Ethiopia, the Kurds, and the Maronites. Were we to factor in the Yemen operation of the mid-1960s (which few were aware of at the time); today's complete or near independence of Iraqi Kurdistan and South Sudan (recognizable as periphery achievements only in retrospect); and Egyptian recognition of Israel's permanence and long strategic reach, which was inspired by Israel's mere proximity to the Blue and White Niles in Africa and is attested to in Arab comments (see chapter 14, "Arab Reaction"), the picture might seem more balanced, even to the skeptics.

Shamir's analysis is important. It constitutes a warning to any Israelis who might be tempted today to put all their eggs in the basket of a new periphery and turn their backs on Turkey and an Islamizing Arab world. Yet by the same token, the analysis is problematic insofar as it finds only drawbacks for Israel on the periphery and ignores achievements and advantages that should appeal even to Israelis who believe opportunities for peace were missed in the past.

One such positive point is that the periphery doctrine never prevented Israel from collaborating secretly with Arab countries, whether Morocco or Jordan, whenever the opportunity arose. With Morocco, incidentally, mediation between Egypt and Israel in 1977 began at Egypt's request and followed years of clandestine cooperation, which included the mass immigration to Israel of Morocco's large Jewish population. In 1977, Egypt's president Sadat also asked the shah of Iran to pass messages to Israel: hardly a zero-sum core–periphery game. As for minorities, Israel's ongoing links with the Kurds and the southern Sudanese hardly point to relationships based exclusively on temporal pragmatism on the part of Israel's partners. Further, the skeptics do not address the Arab world's constant inclination to view Jews and other minorities as, in the best case, protected factions (*dhimmi*) deserving of second-class citizenship, and certainly not as peoples worthy of independence.

There is a problematic assumption embedded in the skeptics' analysis that the Arab world is a kind of semi-organic body that Israel has to deal with as a whole. This contention was reinforced during the period of the original periphery doctrine by the Nasserist grip on the Arab world; more recently it may be said to have found expression in the Arab Peace Initiative, an Arab League take-it-or-leave-it peace and normalization offer to Israel.

In this context, the original periphery doctrine—particularly as embodied in ties with outlying Arab countries and more proximate minorities, together with Israel's historic ties with Jordan and periodic feelers toward powerful central Arab powers, such as Egypt and Iraq—may be understood as an Israeli attempt to fragment Arab unanimity and render Arab hostility easier to deal with. In retrospect this strategy appears to have been at least as legitimate, and almost certainly more productive, than an approach based on the contention that Israel should have shunned all non-Arab ties in the Middle East in favor of an all-out attempt to make peace with the likes of Nasser and the Iraqi and Syrian Baathists. That approach, in the eyes of this observer and after weighing all the evidence, was doomed to tragic failure and would have weakened Israel's hand in the business of peacemaking precisely because Jerusalem would have had no identifiable friends in the region to strengthen its deterrent profile and reduce its image of vulnerability.

Finally, in recent years Israel has confronted a very different reality from that described by Shamir with reference to earlier decades. In the past decade or so, the Arab state system has been characterized by multiple instances of fragmentation and weakness in countries such as Iraq, Yemen, Sudan, and Lebanon. After early 2011, this Arab state predicament morphed into the rise of an Islamism that comprises both Arab states and entities—Egypt (where after the events of July 2013 the Muslim Brotherhood was again in the opposition), the Gaza Strip, Iraq, and Tunisia, and perhaps ultimately all or parts of Syria—alongside non-Arab powers, such as Turkey and Iran.

The hostile core is no longer Arab; it is Islamist. It comprises part of the old periphery (Iran and possibly Turkey), and it is geographically diffuse. Accordingly, a new periphery extends farther afield and is primarily non-Islamist or anti-Islamist. In today's Israel, where media and academic discussion of sensitive security issues is far more widespread and uninhibited than it was during Israel's early decades, a new periphery concept certainly should encounter skepticism, to the extent it is perceived to be repeating a mistake associated with the old periphery: overreliance on partners whose motives are essentially short term and even cynical. By the same token, any new periphery strategy should avoid at all costs a zero-sum approach, which Shamir and others associate with the old periphery: shunning opportunities to exploit avenues of coexistence with Israel's immediate Islamist neighbors.

## NOTES

1. Shimon Shamir interview, Tel Aviv, Dec. 26, 2011.
2. E-mail correspondence with Yaakov Sharett, July 11, 2012.
3. Cited by Yosef Heller, "Migbalot HaDiplomatia," review of Documents on Israeli Foreign Policy, vol. 13, 1958–1959, *Haaretz* book review, Apr. 30, 2003 (Hebrew).
4. Halevy interview.
5. Conversation with Matti Steinberg, Nov. 29, 2012.
6. "Iraq and Iran: Imperatives for the US and Israel," speech sponsored by Washington Institute for Near East Policy, Washington, DC, Dec. 10, 1987.
7. Conversation with Dov Tamari, January 8, 2013.
8. Shimon Avivi, "Rotev BeSalat Teimani," *Mabat Malam* 66, June 2013, p. 13 (Hebrew).
9. Thomas L. Friedman, "Israelis, Wary of Islam's Rise, Question Tilt to Iran in War," *New York Times*, Oct. 31, 1987.
10. Alouph Hareven, *Maariv*, Oct. 10, 1980. This article expands Hareven's defense of the periphery doctrine in the Kurdish context.

## Chapter Twelve

# Between Peripheries

*Peace, Isolation, and Islam*

This chapter discusses the strategic events surrounding and involving Israel during approximately three decades—roughly from the early 1980s to 2011—which can be described as "between peripheries." Our emphasis is not on the events themselves, which can fill many additional books. Rather, we are looking for the dynamics and strands of events that took place during those decades that must be understood to appreciate Israel's current dilemmas in confronting the greater Middle Eastern region.

As the original periphery doctrine ground to a halt, Israel expanded its regional horizons. The peace process that began in 1977 peaked during the first half of the 1990s with the Madrid Conference of late 1991, the Oslo breakthrough of 1993, and the multilateral process. At one point, no fewer than seven Arab countries—Egypt, Jordan, Morocco, Tunisia, Mauritania, Oman, and Qatar—had some level of diplomatic representation in Israel. Israel was a regional player, maintaining links with Arabs and non-Arabs, core and periphery, in the region alike (two of the seven were from the core and five from the periphery).

Developments on the international scene contributed substantially to ending Israel's international isolation and boosting its economic prosperity. During the late 1980s and early 1990s, the collapse of the Soviet Union and the First Gulf War, followed by the Madrid and Oslo processes, brought multiple benefits: diplomatic relations with Russia, China, and India as well as the former Soviet satellite states of Central and Eastern Europe; restored relations with the African countries south of the Sahara, which had severed them in 1973; and the migration to Israel from the former Soviet Union of around one million Jews. All these factors combined to enhance Israel's security and deterrent profile and set the Israeli economy on course to a sustained period of growth and integration into global trade as a postindustrial power.

## COMPLEX ISRAEL–ARAB INTERACTION
## REPLACES THE PERIPHERY

Most Israel–Arab interaction after the classic periphery period touched in some way on the Palestinian issue. In 1982, an attempt by a Likud-led government to place a doubtful periphery ally, the Maronites, in power in Lebanon and in so doing to "Palestinize" Jordan by forcing Lebanon's Palestinians and the PLO leadership to move there—thereby ostensibly freeing Israel to hold on to the West Bank—ended in disaster for Israel, leaving it to combat guerilla attacks in southern Lebanon and northern Israel for another eighteen years. This also signaled at least a partial discrediting of Defense Minister Ariel Sharon's "Jordan is Palestine" scheme.

During the 1980s, when the attention of much of the Middle East was distracted by the Iran–Iraq War, there was little progress on the Palestinian front despite the mandate provided by the 1978 Camp David accords between Israel and Egypt. The reasons were a combination of domestic Israeli political gridlock between right and left and the unavailability of an acceptable Palestinian partner, as the PLO still held to a refusal to countenance Israel's existence.

The first intifada (1987–1992) helped push Israel into a greater readiness to accommodate Palestinian demands. The Madrid conference of December 1991—brought about by the First Gulf War and the collapse of the Soviet Union—created new peace tracks, both bilateral and multilateral, and generated two years of dynamic negotiations that eventually catalyzed the Oslo accords, which brought the Palestine Liberation Organization into the process and paved the way for Israeli–Jordanian peace in 1994.

Despite, or alongside, the various multilateral forums that operated during the early 1990s and the intermittent Israeli–Syrian peace track, the Palestinian issue remained central to the peace concept of most Arab states and the international community. Indeed, by the mid-1990s the failure to register significant progress toward a solution beyond the Oslo agreements became instrumental in radically slowing down the Israel–Arab multilateral relationship and cooling Israeli–Jordanian and Israeli–Egyptian ties. The outbreak of a second intifada in 2000, following a failed Israeli–Palestinian–US peace summit at Camp David, set the scene for another decade of failed negotiations, punctuated by a controversial unilateral Israeli withdrawal from the Gaza Strip in 2005 and the takeover of Gaza in 2007 by the Palestinian Islamist movement Hamas.

Apropos Islamists, the serious exceptions to the broadly positive multilateral dynamics of the early 1990s were Iran's ongoing hostility after 1979 and the emergence in territories under Israel's control, and eventually on its borders, of two militant movements, Hezbollah and Hamas, with strong links to Iran. If "classic" state-versus-state Israel–Arab warfare—characterized by World War II–style armor and air battles—ended with the 1973 war, its successor was asymmetric warfare waged by nonstate actors and featuring attacks on Israel's civilian population by suicide bombers and rockets, coupled with the threat posed by Iran's nuclear program and Tehran's regional hegemonic ambitions.

The Israeli rear became vulnerable for the first time since the 1948 War of Independence. Large budgetary allotments and US military aid grants were invested in interceptor systems to counter incoming rockets and missiles targeting Israel's civilian population. Fences began to go up around Israel's borders, in one case, inside the West Bank, in some ways creating a new virtual border. The Arab states no longer called for Israel's destruction and no longer presented a credible threat of all-out war, thereby radically reducing the sense of existential danger. On the other hand, the Islamists—Iran, Hamas, Hezbollah—did threaten to destroy Israel and did find ways to target a growing segment of Israeli civilian society, yet by and large without posing any immediate existential threat.

Vestiges of the periphery doctrine lived on during the 1980s and 1990s and into the new millennium in the form of generally close and militarily productive strategic relations with Turkey and Ethiopia. The emergence of peaceful relations between Israel and Arab neighbors—whether peace treaties with Jordan and Egypt or the Oslo accords with the PLO and the subsequent creation of the Palestinian Authority—may have minimized the importance of the periphery, but Israel also encountered as those relations developed, the limits of peace and the difficulty of normalizing its relations with the Arabs.

## NO NORMALIZATION

One striking example was the Middle East–North Africa economic summits held in Casablanca, Morocco, from October 30 to November 1, 1994, and in Amman, Jordan, from October 29 to 31, 1995. Israel's enthusiasm for these conferences was based on the assumption that the Madrid multilateral working groups, the Oslo accords of 1993, and the Israeli–Jordanian peace of 1994, all following upon peace with Egypt more than a decade earlier, constituted the point of departure for a "warm" peace. These economic summits were supposed to crystallize and culminate the entire Madrid- and Oslo-born peace process of the 1990s.

Accordingly, Israeli diplomats, economists, and businesspeople descended on these conferences with thick briefing books brimming with economically beneficial joint infrastructure and other projects that would link Israel with its Arab neighbors. Foreign Minister Shimon Peres got so carried away that he declared, "Israel's next goal is to join the Arab League." With very few exceptions, these initiatives were rebuffed, and the joint infrastructure projects proposed in Casablanca and Amman were never implemented. The Arab world was prepared to coexist with Israel but was not interested in an Israeli economic or political presence within its institutions. The Israeli diplomats with their briefing books were termed "neocolonialist," "imperialist," and "arrogant" by Arab media.

A parallel instance of Arab rejection of normalization involved the Arab world's reaction to serious Israeli proposals during the 1990s and early years of the new millennium concerning land swaps involving Israel, Jordan, Egypt, and Syria. The proposals came from senior officials such as Uzi Arad and Giora Eiland, each of whom served as head of Israel's national security staff. The strategic rationale for these initiatives was to advance the cause of Israel–Arab peace treaties by assuring Israel's territorial strategic needs while maintaining the principle of land for peace.

For example, Arad proposed that Israel cede territory to Jordan, Jordan transfer land to Syria, and Syria allow Israel to hold on to an equivalent parcel of the Golan so that Israeli withdrawal within the framework of an Israeli–Syrian peace treaty would not comprise the militarily important escarpment overlooking Lake Kinneret (the Sea of Galilee). Eiland proposed that Israel cede the territory in the Negev to Egypt, which would facilitate easier Egyptian territorial access to Jordan and the Arab east. In return, Egypt would allow the Palestinians to expand the Gaza Strip into the northeastern Sinai Peninsula, thereby alleviating Gaza's demographic pressures without obliging Israel to expand the Gaza Strip into its own territory as part of an Israeli–Palestinian two-state solution.

Both Arad and Eiland pointed out that Arab states had themselves been dealing with their border issues during the second half of the twentieth century by swapping territory. Egypt and Sudan, Jordan and Saudi Arabia, and Jordan and Iraq had all done so. Why shouldn't Arab countries swap land with Israel, too?

Arguably, these proposals represented a refusal to come to terms with the straightforward requirement of the Israeli–Palestinian peace process that the conflict be resolved within the territorial boundaries of Mandatory Palestine, without involving Israel's other neighbors territorially. Many Israelis and others familiar with the Palestinian and general Arab positions recognized that the proposals were futile. Yet the tenor and depth of the Arab refusal to countenance these ideas was both stunning and instructive.

(There are two limited exceptions to this refusal. Jordan swapped territories with Israel in the context of the two countries' bilateral peace agreement in 1994. And the Palestine Liberation Organization has agreed in principle to territorial swaps that would enable Israel to hold on to settlement blocs in the West Bank if and when the two parties agree on a two-state solution. But neither Jordan nor the PLO has agreed to the three-way swaps discussed here. In the course of Israeli–Egyptian peace negotiations in the late 1970s, Egypt refused to exchange land so as to leave Taba on the Red Sea coast under Israeli control.)

The derisive Arab response these proposals usually elicited plainly reflected an Arab perception that Israel was not "a member of the family" and could not engage in such territorial exercises with its Arab neighbors or move deeper into the Arab sphere as if it were. The Arab Peace Initiative of March 2002 is a case in point: it offers comprehensive normal relations, but only after comprehensive peace. The logic of this position is clear and understandable, even if many Israelis doubt whether a two-state solution with the Palestinians would really expand the parameters of Arab coexistence with Israel. But that logic cannot be understood to apply to the instances cited here, wherein most of the Arab world invites Israel to an economic conference or Israel suggests land swaps precisely to facilitate peace with Syria or the Palestinians.

The author had a similar experience in working in the course of twelve years prior to 2013 as the Israeli coeditor of the bitterlemons-international.org publications, which brought together Israeli, Arab, Iranian, Turkish, and other writers to address specific Middle Eastern issues. I suggested to bitterlemons' Palestinian coeditor Ghassan Khatib that an internationally recognized Israeli expert on a relatively little-studied Arab country such as Libya or Sudan could be invited to address a Libyan or Sudanese issue that does not touch on Israel, such as illegal migration to Europe from Libya or the Darfur issue in Sudan. We had encountered considerable difficulty finding Arab experts on these subjects and simply needed writers. As was customary when the topic involved Israel and an Arab country, the Israeli writer would appear on the same virtual page with Arab writers analyzing the topic.

Khatib's reply was firmly in the negative. For a joint Arab–Israel project to allow an Israeli to discuss the internal affairs of an Arab country that had no Israeli link or context would constitute "normalization," he asserted. Without a comprehensive end to the conflict, this would be unacceptable to Arabs and render the bitterlemons' project unacceptable to them. Whether he was right is not the issue: this is the reality and extent of Israel–Arab interaction. Incidentally, one of the main reasons we eventually closed bitterlemons at the height of the Arab revolutions in 2012 was the growing refusal of Arabs in general, including Palestinians, to collaborate with a joint Israeli–Palestinian Internet project whose product is universally accessible by writing for us, even when no Israeli writers were involved.

## DISCOVERING THE LIMITATIONS OF PEACE

The significance of this brief discussion lies in its relevance for Israeli attitudes toward Arab neighbors as opposed to non-Arab neighbors. From 1977 until today, Israelis have discovered both the advantages and limitations of peace with Arab neighbors. The advantages are strategic and even existential in the military sense. Since the late 1970s there has been essentially no danger of war with Egypt—even Egypt under a Muslim Brotherhood president—and by extension, as noted above, with a hostile Arab coalition.

The limitations concern anything smacking of normalization, such as a warm welcome for mass Israeli tourism or major open and public energy deals. These transactions can happen with non-Arab Azerbaijan and Cyprus and possibly even Islamist-governed Turkey (see chapter 13, "Is There a New Periphery?"), but almost certainly not with Egypt. (Cairo did briefly sell natural gas to Israel prior to the 2011 revolution in a deal roundly condemned by many quarters of Egyptian society, which was canceled after the fall of Hosni Mubarak, and then undertook in 2014 to import gas from Israel, in yet another highly controversial move.) Moreover, to the extent that countries from the region can be induced to enter into a partnership with Israel that is directed against the activities of another country in the region, Israel's counterparts are peripheral in the ethnic and geographic sense. They are not likely to be from the Arab core, where cooperation with Egypt and Jordan focuses on issues of terrorism and extremist Islam.

In recent years, Egypt and Israel have moved closer to one another regarding regional concerns. Egypt has attempted to mediate between Israel and Gaza-based Hamas and additional Islamist extremists in Gaza and in July 2014 even tilted toward Israel in its war with Islamist Hamas. Peace with Jordan provides crucial strategic depth to Israel's east and a quiet border. Beginning in 2013, it has been directed against jointly perceived threats emanating from the revolution in Syria.[1] Israel may see eye to eye with Saudi Arabia and the United Arab Emirates on major issues such as Iran and militant Islam, but it would be far fetched to suggest there is any sort of open partnership between the two.

Even before the "Arab spring," during the first decade of the new millennium, the entire Israel–Arab normalization and interaction issue was dwarfed by the perception of disfunctionality among a large number of Arab countries. In Lebanon, Iraq, Sudan, Yemen, the Palestinian Authority, and Somalia (the latter an Arab League member albeit not an Arab country) the central government, if there was one, no longer controlled all the state's territory.

The era of Arab revolution and anarchy that began in 2011 may have over-shadowed this reality, but the two phenomena are almost certainly related. Moreover, in combination they reduce the attractiveness of Arab countries as partners for commercial, cultural, or political interaction, and not only with Israel. Then too, the rising influence of the Arab "street" since 2011 means that Arab leaders are more attuned to public opinion, which is frequently Islamist in nature. Ostensibly, this means they have less latitude and flexibility than previously with regard to their relations with Israel, though in 2014 both Egypt and Jordan were so concerned with militant Islamist threats that they constituted exceptions to this apparent rule.

In looking at the benefits and limitations of Israel–Arab peace, the Israeli–US relationship is of prime importance. Throughout the latter part of the periphery period and the entire time since then and to this day, strategic ties between Washington and Jerusalem have remained a key foundation of Israel's entire approach to the region. The tragic 9/11 al-Qaeda terrorist attacks on the United States and the subsequent US invasions of Afghanistan and Iraq enhanced those traditional ties and augmented a sense of shared interests and a shared enemy in the Middle East. In examining US public opinion, the attitude of powerful pro-Israel sectors of the US population, such as the Jewish and evangelical communities, and the readiness of the US security community to work in close concert with Israel, there is every indication that this foundation will remain solid.

Certainly, the Israeli–US alliance has held firm in recent years as a succession of Arab regimes—including two, Egypt and Tunisia, considered moderate and close to the United States—have undergone radical revolutionary change, which has at least temporarily brought to the fore diverse expressions of political Islam: primarily the Muslim Brotherhood and Salafist movements. Yet in 2014 the United States was also clearly executing a calculated distancing or withdrawal from conflicts in the region, such as in Syria; from upheavals in friendly countries, such as in Egypt; and even from conflicts in neighboring areas, such as in Ukraine—a distancing that could conceivably have far-reaching ramifications even for Israeli–US relations and that was exacerbated by US policy failures in the Israeli–Palestinian sphere in 2013–2014: first, to facilitate a renewed peace process and second, to promote a quick conclusion to the Israeli–Hamas war of July 2014.

## A NEW RING OF HOSTILITY?

Israel today increasingly sees itself ringed by Islamists wielding or threatening to seize political power and who are more hostile to it and its very existence than were the secular regimes they displaced or the ones they aspire to replace. Beyond falling back on the support of the United States as it partially withdraws from the region, Israel has to develop new strategic options for dealing with this challenge.

Where is the challenge? Beginning on Israel's southwest border, during 2012–2013 Israel encountered a Muslim Brotherhood–ruled Egypt, which maintained its peace agreement with Israel thanks largely to pressure from the West and the Egyptian military. But it at least temporarily ceded partial control of the Sinai Peninsula bordering Israel to Salafist elements. While Israel and Egypt did continue to hold security consultations concerning the situation in Sinai, until the Egyptian army deposed the Muslim Brotherhood government in Cairo in July 2013, the army was constrained in its freedom to confront the Salafists with force. Even after the army's coup, it confronted violent Islamist opposition in Sinai and the Egyptian heartland. By mid-2014, extreme demographic and economic conditions rendered Egypt's Islamists a potent residual element in terms of influencing regional stability.

The Gaza Strip has been under Hamas rule—effectively, the Palestinian branch of the Muslim Brotherhood—since 2007. By 2014 Salafist forces were on the rise there too, and Egypt's army rulers tended to view Gaza's Islamists as a hostile extension of Egypt's own Islamists.

Continuing around the map of Israel's neighbors, Hezbollah, representing extreme Shi'ite Islam, has confronted Israel from southern Lebanon, with active Iranian and Syrian support, since 1983. The chaos in Syria had begun by 2013 to generate both a Sunni Salafi threat and a Hezbollah threat on Israel's Golan border. The chaotic situation in southern Syria mounted a growing challenge to the moderate rule of King Abdullah II in Jordan. Under these circumstances—and completing the circle of its borders—Israel had understandable concerns about the capacity of the non-Islamist Palestine Liberation Organization to maintain its rule over the West Bank, particularly if Israeli forces were to withdraw under the terms of some sort of Israeli–Palestinian peace process.

Add to this "Islamist ring" the hostility of Turkey and Iran—Israel's periphery partners against Arab enmity in the past—and the perception of a new ring of hostility loomed large by 2013. Even the beginnings of Israeli–Turkish rapprochement in the spring of 2013 and the anti-Islamist coup in Egypt in mid-2013 could not entirely dispel this notion. It was nourished no longer by Nasserism and Arab nationalism as in the 1950s and 1960s, but rather by political Islam. The threats the Islamist ring presented were, at least for the near future, not conventional warfare but nuclear blackmail (Iran) and asymmetric terrorism (Hezbollah, Hamas, Salafists) backed by Islamist regimes in Iran and conceivably in Syria. It projected the specter of regional isolation for Israel.

On the other hand, Israel in 2014 is not the country that faced a hostile Arab world in the 1950s and responded with the periphery doctrine. It is a medium-sized country of over eight million inhabitants with a high-tech, postindustrial economy that functions at the global level. It is a military powerhouse that no longer faces the threat of massive conventional warfare. Its economic interaction with the European Union, the United States, and China and its military interaction with NATO and of course the United States are highly developed. Internationally, as opposed to regionally, it is not isolated, maintaining extensive relations, in some cases of a strategic nature, with most of the world's medium and large powers.

Politically, Israel's citizens were in 2014 far more concerned with domestic social and economic issues than with external threats—a dramatic reversal of the reality of past decades. Israel's politics were increasingly dominated by domestic political actors who were not oriented toward peace based on territorial compromise, as well as by otherwise moderate actors who were convinced that Israel had few if any partners for genuine coexistence in the region. In particular, the settler lobby had established a strong presence within dominant political and even security circles and appeared to prefer an apartheid-like state between the Jordan River and the Mediterranean rather than a two-state solution. Further, by 2014 the obvious fact that Israel's policies toward and negative interaction with the Palestinians had lost it considerable popular support in many countries and influential circles had not—or at least, not yet—significantly affected its political and regional behavior. This was clearly reflected in Israel's defiant behavior during the July-August 2014 Gaza war, when civilian casualties in the Gaza Strip generated far-reaching international condemnation of Israeli tactics.

Assuming Israel's global relations remain relatively stable, what are its regional strategic options under these circumstances? Is a new periphery doctrine one of them?

## NOTE

1. Jeffrey Goldberg, *The Atlantic*, Mar. 18, 2013.

## Chapter Thirteen

# Is There a New Periphery?

In the previous chapter we discussed how the original periphery doctrine faded away decades ago. It was superseded in Israel's strategic calculations by the beginnings of peace with the Arabs, the collapse of the Soviet Union and Soviet Bloc, a radical expansion of Israel's international diplomatic and commercial reach, the energetic integration of Israel's robust postindustrial economy into global trade, and massive immigration to Israel from the former Soviet countries.

Classic Israel–Arab wars ended in 1973, to be replaced by asymmetric conflicts and the Iranian nuclear threat. The increasingly dysfunctional nature of Arab regimes over the first decade of the twenty-first century signaled Israel that it had little to fear in the foreseeable future from a coalition of Arab states.

Then came the "Arab spring" revolutions and political Islam—not only on Israel's borders but in the former periphery as well. Israel has recognized the possibility that it could again be surrounded by a ring of hostile states constituting an even larger core than in the past: Islamist regimes in Arab entities and states as well as in Turkey and Iran.

Thus has commenced a process, in security and government circles as well as in think tanks, of discussing the feasibility and viability of a new periphery that would be designed to outflank, balance, and deter the Islamist forces gathering around Israel. Discussion of this challenge is rendered particularly problematic by the rapid pace of events in the Middle East. In 2010 new-periphery thinking did not exist. In the ensuing years, under the shadow of Islam in Turkey and Egypt, it flourished. After the Mavi Marmara apology and the overthrow of the Muslim Brotherhood in Egypt in 2013, the issue appeared less urgent and far more diffuse. Because new-periphery countries often could not be defined as peripheral geographically and Islamist core countries were not constant, strategic planners in the Prime Minister's Office and the foreign and defense ministries[1] have employed guarded terms such as "circles of containment," "axes of containment," "new periphery architecture," and "arcs."

As the presumed hostile core has grown, the resultant periphery extends well beyond the Middle East. The new periphery is generally understood to comprise at its core Azerbaijan to the north of Iran, Greece and Cyprus vis-à-vis Turkey, and Ethiopia and South Sudan—representing continuity with the original periphery—to the south of Egypt and Sudan. The Gulf emirates are also usually mentioned.

A more expansive approach would also include Kenya and Uganda in East Africa, Morocco in North Africa, and Iraqi Kurdistan—again, continuity with the past—as well as two European states north of Turkey—Bulgaria and Romania. There is also a new and interesting phenomenon of North African Berbers taking an interest in ties with Israel in an effort to distinguish themselves from the Arab establishment in countries such as Morocco and Algeria.

A very early effort to describe a new periphery, by former Deputy Minister of Defense Ephraim Sneh in 1996, spotlighted among other countries Azerbaijan and Eritrea, alongside Turkey, the Maghreb, the Kurds, and the then newly independent countries of Central Asia.[2] Indeed, at that time it was possible to describe a new northern triangle comprising Israel, Azerbaijan, and Turkey.[3] A recent high-level academic attempt to reformulate Israel's national security strategy suggests three regions where Israel is advised to promote formal and informal alliances: the eastern Mediterranean, with emphasis on Greece and Cyprus; Saudi Arabia and some of the emirates; and East Africa—Ethiopia, Kenya, South Sudan, and Uganda.[4]

In the pages that follow, we look at Israel's main new periphery partners based on their geographic locations and the strategic functions they serve from Israel's standpoint. We do so in full recognition that there is ambiguity here, both geographically and politically. Neither Turkey nor Egypt can be straightforwardly identified as Islamist core. Cyprus can hardly be considered geographic periphery, when it is closer to Israel than to Turkey, the country it ostensibly contains, in a periphery sense. Obviously, the concept of a new periphery or spheres of containment loses much of its strategic rationale to the extent that Turkey and Egypt do not pose an Islamist threat to Israel.

Moreover, at a time (2013–2014) when Turkish trucks bearing goods for the Arab world have been rerouted away from their traditional transit route via Syria—where war renders the trip too dangerous—and are instead transported by ship to the Israeli port of Haifa, from where they drive across Israel into Jordan and on to the Gulf, the notion of outflanking, or containing,

Turkey has to be understood as projecting a strategy that, however significant, is also of limited relevance.

## CYPRUS, GREECE, AND THE "TURKISH PERIPHERY"

Of all the countries bordering on Turkey with which Israel has tightened ties in recent years, Cyprus and Greece stand out. Israel has also developed military and intelligence ties with Bulgaria and Romania to the north of Turkey, including joint air force exercises in both countries.[5] An unusual photo op of Mossad head Meir Dagan and Prime Minister Boyko Borisov of Bulgaria in late October 2010, shortly after the Mavi Marmara incident had led to serious deterioration in Israeli–Turkish relations, may have been intended to impress Turkey that Israel was well positioned on its northern flank: Since when do chiefs of the Mossad pose for press photos with regional heads of state?[6] But it is the Mediterranean periphery arena, meaning Cyprus and Greece, with its proximity to Israel and its energy potential, that remains central. In the spring of 2014, Israeli foreign minister Avigdor Lieberman was described as a devoted advocate of a "bypass-Ankara axis," which centers on Greece and Cyprus.[7]

In recent years, Israel has developed a military and intelligence cooperation relationship with both Athens and Nicosia, alongside an energy cooperation relationship with Cyprus, which could be expanded to include Greece. One key component of these ties is shared concern over Turkey's turn toward an Islamist orientation and to a lesser extent over Arab Islamism and Islamist terrorism. Another is the need to secure potentially lucrative neighboring and jointly developed gas exploration and production facilities in the eastern Mediterranean against possible threats not only from Turkey but also from terrorist actors based in the region. In the case of Greece, concern over problematic Muslim immigration is another motivating factor for moving closer strategically to Israel.

The security issues at stake in the eastern Mediterranean energy context are complex and tend to reinforce the perception that Cyprus has little alternative but to look to Israel for security where its energy interests and to some extent its relationship with Turkey—regarding energy as well as the veteran Cyprus dispute—are concerned.[8]

Both Cyprus and Israel are at loggerheads with Lebanon as well on the energy front. Israel's EEZ (exclusive economic zone, a maritime delineation) border with Lebanon, its neighbor to the north, is in dispute. Lebanon and Israel are officially at war and maintain no direct diplomatic or economic contacts. Leaders of Hezbollah—a militant Shi'ite movement and ally of Iran, whose forces are deployed in southern Lebanon, Beirut, the Beqaa Valley, and even since 2013, Syria—have alternately recognized the need to resolve the dispute peacefully so that the Lebanese can profit economically from their own gas exploration and threatened the use of force against Israel, going so far as to boast of possessing the means to attack Israeli maritime energy installations.

Nor would an unresolved Israeli–Lebanese dispute over drilling rights be confined necessarily to those two countries. While Lebanon and Cyprus have delineated their EEZ border, by 2014 that agreement had still not been ratified by the Lebanese parliament due to fear of Turkey's response. Moreover, Lebanon links its dispute with Israel to Palestinian energy claims off the Gaza coast, seeking to paint Israel as stealing Arab natural resources. Since the Hamas takeover of the Gaza Strip in 2007, Israel has effectively prevented Palestinian maritime drilling, citing both security considerations and the international boycott of Hamas.

Syria could also become a Mediterranean gas producer if and when sovereign tranquility is restored and exploration begins. Any regime in Damascus would presumably line up with Lebanon regarding its EEZ disputes with Israel and Cyprus.

Cyprus' territorial dispute with Turkey, centering on the Turkish Republic of Northern Cyprus, which Turkey carved out in its 1974 invasion, has taken on a maritime dimension that potentially dwarfs the Israeli–Lebanese dispute. Turkey challenges the Cypriot EEZ and map of drilling zones, claiming that a portion of the gas must be assigned to the Turkish Republic of Northern Cyprus (TRNC). In effect, it demands that Cyprus share either with it or with Northern Cyprus. Turkey's claims on Cyprus' Aphrodite field and other drilling sites reportedly led to violations of Cypriot waters by the Turkish navy in May 2012, with both Israel and Turkey deploying military aircraft.

Cyprus appears to view its commercial partnership with Israel and Israeli companies, as well as its strong links with Russia and its membership in the European Union (including preferential allocation of drilling sites in the Cyprus EEZ), as a potential guarantee of the security of its gas exploration vis-à-vis Turkey. Israeli prime minister Benjamin Netanyahu visited Cyprus in February 2012—a visit that generated rumors concerning possible Israel Air Force use of bases in Cyprus, which has no air force of its own. "Cyprus feels it can rely on Israel from a security standpoint" is a sentiment heard both in Cypriot energy circles and the Israeli Prime Minister's Office.[9] In May 2013, newly elected Cypriot president Nicos Anastasiades visited Israel and termed it a "strategic partner."[10]

Later that same month, Greek foreign minister Dimitris Avramopoulos also visited Israel for talks about strategic cooperation. Greece, too, seeks to drill for gas and oil in the eastern Mediterranean and Aegean Seas. Its potential for EEZ and maritime disputes with Turkey has always been volatile, and in early 2013 it was still delaying maritime drilling. The Greek and Israeli navies and air forces have in recent years conducted joint exercises, and in 2010 Greek prime minister George Papandreou and Netanyahu exchanged visits. Israel, Greece, and Cyprus are also collaborating with regard to developing infrastructures for natural gas exports to Europe and for a shared electricity grid.

This, along with successful Israeli collaboration with Cyprus, Greece, and even Egypt regarding delineation of EEZs, appears to have left Turkey poorly positioned to press its case regarding Mediterranean energy issues. Any improvement in Israeli–Turkish relations following Israel's March 2013 apology to Turkey over the May 2010 Mavi Marmara incident could conceivably reduce tensions over Mediterranean gas and upgrade discussions of a seabed pipeline linking Israel's gas fields to Turkey,[11] but it is not likely to appreciably reduce tensions emanating from Turkey's Islamist outlook or between Turkey and Cyprus.[12]

Cyprus and Greece were not always so inclined to rely on Israel's military might as a deterrent against Turkish meddling. Cyprus has a long tradition, going back to independence under Archbishop Makarios III in 1960, of association with the nonaligned movement, which brought it into close contact with the Arab world. It also has a vibrant communist movement, which once took its cue from the Soviet Union; it now hosts numerous Russian and Ukrainian offshore economic enterprises. Israel was also long looked upon by Nicosia with suspicion due to its close ties with Turkey.

But there is no longer a Soviet Union, the nonaligned movement has far less international relevance than it did in the 1960s, the Islamizing Arab world is increasingly associated with Turkey, and since 2004 Cyprus has been a member of the European Union. Still, in Cypriot foreign policy circles there is lingering sentiment for closer Arab ties and commercial and security reliance on Russia. Moscow, according to some assessments, could conceivably view an energy alliance with Cyprus and Israel as an alternative foothold in the Middle East if and when it is forced to abandon its presence in Bashar al-Assad's Syria.[13] Some Cypriots still view the Arab world as an important buffer for Cyprus against Turkish pressures over the TRNC.

So the Israeli–Cypriot relationship could hardly be termed a solid alliance. That Cypriot officials felt they had alternatives, or at least wanted Israel to think so, was made plain in November 2012 when I met with Solon Kassinis in his Nicosia office. Kassinis is director of the Energy Service at the Cypriot Ministry of Commerce, Industry and Tourism. He is the official in charge of Cyprus' gas exploration and production in the Mediterranean. As such, he works closely with his Israeli counterparts in coordinating gas-related issues, such as joint investment in liquid natural gas (LNG) facilities and pipelines, the glue that holds together the new Israeli–Cypriot strategic relationship.

He was in an angry mood when I met him. Israel's energy industry, he complained, was overbureaucratized. It kept him waiting years for decisions. "Don't you Israelis understand that we're the only friends you have?" he blurted out in frustration. "That's it, Greece and Cyprus. We're not afraid of Turkey; we don't need Israel for that. Israel needs Cyprus. So either the three of us agree on issues of gas security or we'll protect our gas exploration with help from Russia, France and Italy."

I'd been briefed that Kassinis had a reputation for bluster and bluff, but his point of view was interesting: in his eyes, and presumably those of additional Cypriots and Greeks, Israel is all alone. True, it can provide security for Mediterranean gas exploration and installation projects against Turkey's threats—security that Cyprus and Greece cannot provide—but Israelis should be more appreciative of the few friends they have, because those friends could conceivably have alternative options. One could infer from Kassinis's remark that Israel had not done enough to infuse its relationship with Cyprus with a shared strategic dimension. Or was this simply Byzantine bluff?

Greece, for its part, has long had close Arab ties; Athens elevated its diplomatic relations with Israel to ambassadorial level only in 1990, as the communist bloc was collapsing. In recent years, with the rise of an Islamist government in Turkey, Greek elites have become more pro-Israel in orientation, with some explaining that Greece can adopt a tougher stance vis-à-vis Turkey thanks to Israeli military backing.

Yet the Greek approach toward close collaboration with Israel, even more than that of Cyprus, is infused with second thoughts and ambiguities. On the one hand, people such as Gerasimos Arsenis, who as Greek minister of defense in 1994 executed a brief strategic opening to Israel, which was then mothballed until 2010 by the pro-Arab faction in Athens, continue to believe in the viability of "the meeting of Hellenic and Israeli security zones." A variety of Greek academic experts recognize the contribution Israel's US connections, and particularly the pro-Israel lobby in Washington, can make toward strengthening the Greek lobby in the United States and possibly helping Greece with its finances, but they fear lest Israeli–Greek ties damage oil supplies to Greece from Iran and constrain Athens' access to Greek Orthodox communities in the Levant. They recognize that Israel needs a close relationship with Turkey but wonder whether Jerusalem can balance close relations with both Ankara and Athens.

A very senior Greek journalist, in a conversation in April 2013, listed two additional fears among the Greek political leadership regarding the direction of relations with Israel. One is violent reaction by Greece's growing Muslim migrant population against Athens' cooperation with Israel. Some one million Muslims have arrived in recent years from Pakistan, North Africa, and Albania and are largely unabsorbed into Greek society.

A second concern is what the journalist termed the excesses of Israeli bravado. Senior Israeli officials have in recent years offered security assurances to Athens—for example, in the form of joint defense plans—which leave Greek leaders at one and the same time lulled into a false sense of security regarding frictions with Turkey and concerned lest their ties with Israel drag them into conflict.[14] On the other hand, Israeli officials indicate that on at least one occasion Greece tried to induce Israel to stage joint naval exercises in areas where sovereignty is disputed with Turkey.

Beyond military strategic issues, as of 2013–2014 a key economic constraint on the capacity of Israel, Cyprus, and Greece to develop a network of energy links was the financial crisis that plagued the latter two countries. A second constraint was Egypt's decision in mid-2014 to purchase gas from Israel's Mediterranean deposits, which reflected a radical revision of Cairo's regional priorities—one welcomed by Israel—and could significantly reduce Israel's need to market gas via Cyprus and Greece.

## AZERBAIJAN

Israel recognized Azerbaijan's strategic importance shortly after Baku achieved independence from the Soviet Union in 1991 and has cultivated the relationship ever since. Initially, Israel's relations with Azerbaijan complemented the Israeli–Turkish strategic relationship in a kind of revived periphery northern triangle: Azeris speak a dialect of Turkish and the two countries are close. The Israeli–Azeri link has proven important enough to both countries to have survived the sharp deterioration in Israeli–Turkish ties in recent years. Tens of thousands of Jews have emigrated from Azerbaijan to Israel, and Azeri–Jewish ties are considered an integral part of the two countries' relationship.

Azerbaijan borders Iran to that country's north; its population of nine million, mostly secular Shi'ites, is paralleled by a much larger Shi'ite Azeri population, some twenty million strong, in northern Iran. Baku, where an authoritarian regime rules, is sensitive to Iranian incitement of its Shi'ite population as well as to Iranian support for neighboring Armenia, with which Azerbaijan has had a long-running violent dispute over the territory of Nagorno–Karabakh since both countries won independence. On the other hand, Iran is sensitive to irredentist sentiments in Azerbaijan, which characterized the early years of Azeri independence from Moscow.

Israel's strategic interest in Azerbaijan has several aspects, including energy supply. Notwithstanding media exaggerations of the extent of Israeli–Azeri security cooperation, the relationship is obviously a very solid one—"along the dimensions of the periphery of the past," according to a senior Israeli security official. Still, like Israel's Trident partners of old, the

Azeris prefer to keep their ties with Israel discreet. Azerbaijan has never opened an embassy in Israel, and its most senior officials never reciprocated very public visits to Baku by Foreign Minister Avigdor Lieberman, President Shimon Peres, and others until April 2013, when Foreign Minister Elmar Mammadyarov visited Jerusalem.

There is an assumption among senior Israeli security and political circles that Israel's very presence in Azerbaijan is understood by Iran as a deterrent threat. As former Deputy Defense Minister Ephraim Sneh put it, "If we maintain good relations with Azerbaijan then we have an alliance in Iran's back yard or, if you like, in its attic. The map speaks for itself."[15] One Israeli security commentator noted, on the occasion of the Mammadyarov visit, that Tehran "increasingly fears that Azerbaijan is turning into a base" for an Israeli strike against its nuclear facilities.[16]

While there is ample precedent in Iran's tumultuous history for Azeri rebellion, there is no overt and concrete evidence that Iran indeed links the Israeli–Azeri relationship with some new Azeri separatist movement in Iran. On the face of it, this appears to be yet another instance of wishful thinking on the part of the Israeli establishment, based on periphery nostalgia, regarding the potential for destabilizing or antagonizing the Islamic Republic in Tehran.

## ETHIOPIA, SOUTH SUDAN, AND KENYA

Israel's strategic ties in the Horn of Africa and East Africa have traditionally focused on two security fronts: countering radical Arab and Islamic influence and countering Egypt's sway in the region. This second front has metamorphosed with the vicissitudes of Israel's peace with Egypt: from direct confrontation with Nasserist Egypt in the 1960s, to countering Egyptian attempts to dissuade African states from warming relations with Israel even after Egypt and Israel signed a peace treaty in 1979, to cultivating key relationships in anticipation of possible further deterioration in an Egypt where the Muslim Brotherhood has become a key political actor.

Regardless of these developments, Israel's strategic ties in the region have remained relatively steady over the years and represent a high degree of continuity. This is particularly so regarding security ties with Ethiopia and Kenya and to a lesser extent with Uganda. South Sudan, an independent state since 2011, has welcomed ties with Israel, almost as if the Israeli aid effort to the Anya Nya southern Sudanese independence movement did not end in 1972. Israel is providing aid to South Sudan in the field of water infrastructure and technology, and Israeli oil companies are interested in drilling in South Sudan and possibly participating in laying an oil pipeline via Kenya to the Indian Ocean to free South Sudan of its problematic reliance on Sudan to its north for exporting its oil.[17] By 2014 Israeli–South Sudanese affinity was marred only by the disastrous effect on South Sudan's sovereign viability of tribal civil war in that country.

Security cooperation is central. In November 2011, Prime Minister Raila Odinga of Kenya and President Yoweri Museveni of Uganda visited Israel simultaneously, against a backdrop of gathering concern in their countries over penetration by forces of radical Islam.[18] In 2010 the *Economist* noted that "security-minded Ethiopia, confronting Islamist militias backed by near-by rebels in Somalia, has become Israel's closest continental ally and a big buyer of defence equipment."[19] In 2014 Israeli foreign minister Lieberman, a strong "new periphery" advocate, spearheaded an upgrading of Israel's rela-tions with a host of African countries in the Sahel and farther south, and Israel applied for observer status in the African Union.

Only with Eritrea have strategic ties cooled in recent years, as the Afwer-ki regime in Asmara has isolated itself internationally over human rights issues and the illegal entry into Israel of tens of thousands of Eritreans fleeing their homeland has soured relations. Prior to its hard-fought indepen-dence in 1991, Eritrea was part of Ethiopia, but the Israeli–Eritrean security relationship flourished after independence as well. Today, notwithstanding media exaggerations, the relationship has been downgraded.

Of particular relevance in assessing the contribution of Ethiopia and South Sudan to the new periphery is the Nile River and Egypt's attitude toward Israel's ties with these and additional Nile riparian states. Israel has never in any way sought to tamper with the flow of the Blue Nile from Ethiopia (which accounts for fully 80 percent of the Nile supply to Egypt) or the White Nile from South Sudan and countries farther south. Chinese and Italian firms, not Israeli, are building the massive Grand Ethiopian Renais-sance Dam for generating hydropower on the Blue Nile in Ethiopia, which has caused such concern in Cairo. Yet, as we shall see in looking at Arab responses to the periphery doctrine (chapter 14), Egypt is so existentially obsessed with guaranteeing the Nile flow that serious Egyptian strategic thinkers, as well as the more sensationalistic press, have persisted even in recent years in searching for an invisible Israeli hand that is somehow divert-ing Egypt's water supply.[20]

In this way, an imaginary Israeli role has been injected into the controver-sy between Egypt and the African Nile riparian states over the distribution of Nile waters. In the extreme event of conflict between Egypt and Ethiopia over the dam issue (with Sudan, which surprisingly supports the Ethiopian position, caught in the middle), Israel could find itself in an uncomfortable position insofar as it enjoys a close relationship with Ethiopia. Here is an area where Israel can proactively reassure Egypt regarding its pure intentions, perhaps via a third party and conceivably as part of a confidence-building package between the two countries. Conceivably, too, if and as Israeli–Egyptian relations flower as a buffer against militant Islamists in the region, Israel's expertise in desalinating and recycling water could be useful to Egypt and could enhance Egyptian–Ethiopian relations by reducing the extent of Egypt's water shortage.

## THE EMIRATES

Most of Israel's ties with the Persian Gulf emirates began with the Madrid peace conference of December 1991. In the ensuing five years, Israelis sat down with representatives of some fifteen Arab countries, including those from the Gulf, within the framework of the five working groups of the Madrid multilateral peace process. Several of the emirates, including Qatar and Oman (with which Israel had a previous clandestine relationship) exchanged low-level diplomatic representatives with Israel. Out of this interaction, and despite the demise of the official multilateral process in 1995–1996, commercial and political relationships developed, which exist to this day.

Oman expelled Israel's diplomats in 2000 and Qatar, in 2009. Each country cited the Palestinian issue as the cause. On the other hand, Israel reportedly opened a diplomatic office in late 2011 or early 2012 in a Gulf state; this fact was revealed inadvertently by the finance ministry on its website in 2013. And in July 2013 the Israeli Foreign Ministry opened a "virtual embassy" on a Twitter account directed toward dialogue with Saudi Arabia and the Gulf emirates.[21] In February 2013, Israel's president Shimon Peres addressed a convocation in Abu Dhabi of twenty-nine foreign ministers from the emirates, the Arab League, and Muslim states via a conference call from Jerusalem.[22] In recent years, in particular, a key reinforcing factor is shared concern about Iran's regional designs and allegations of Iranian incitement of Shi'ite communities in the Gulf Arab states. In 2014, the threat posed by the Sunni extremist movement ISIS or the "Islamic State" in the Levant and Iraq, and Israel's war with Hamas in Gaza, reportedly further enhanced Israeli–UAE and Israeli–Saudi strategic cooperation.

## MOROCCO AND THE BERBERS

As described in chapter 3, discrete Israeli–Moroccan relations have continued since the demise of the broader periphery doctrine in the late 1970s and early 1980s. The 1991 Madrid peace conference, followed by the Oslo process between Israel and the Palestine Liberation Organization and the multilateral working groups, ushered in an era of official low-level diplomatic relations, beginning in 1994 and ending in 2000 with the outbreak of the second intifada. Prime Minister Shimon Peres paid an official visit in 1986, followed by Prime Minister Yitzhak Rabin in September 1993 on his way back to Israel from the Oslo signing in Washington.

During the flourishing of the multilateral era, Israel and more than a dozen Arab countries participated in meetings held in Morocco. Israeli tourism to Morocco continues to this day. While Morocco no longer aspires to play a significant role in mediating broader Israel–Arab ties, a new Moroccan constitution promulgated in the era of the "Arab spring" assigns a unique role to the country's Jewish heritage, and a unique role to the country's Berber, or Amazigh, heritage.[23] In recent years portions of the Amazigh in Morocco, who constitute around 40 percent of the population, and their fellow Berbers, or Kabyles, in Algeria (about 20 percent of the population), have developed a Berber ethnocultural identity movement among North Africa's indigenous or pre-Arab population. Theories have proliferated as far afield as postrevolutionary Libya regarding the Berbers' Jewish origins or, alternatively, intermixing between Jews and Berbers in the pre-Arab period. In November 2009, an Amazigh delegation participated in a seminar in Jerusalem at Israel's Yad Vashem memorial to the Holocaust.

In some ways this Berber awakening—as an expression of minority rejection of Arab hegemony—reflected the weakening of the Arab state system, for example, in Libya, which characterized the years preceding the Arab revolutionary wave, which began in early 2011. New, liberalized ethnic policies in Algeria and particularly Morocco allowed the movement to operate even earlier. Since the Arab revolutions and the rise of an Islamist movement in Morocco, the Amazighs have been targeted there because of their alleged sympathy for Israel.[24]

The Amazigh cannot be defined as an active part of an ethnic periphery or of an Israeli minority policy. Israeli outreach toward them is minimal. Their cultural renewal is not known to be a negative factor in Israeli–Moroccan relations. Still, any survey of the new periphery cannot completely ignore them.

## THE KURDS OF NORTHERN IRAQ

A close and virtually exclusive Israeli–Kurdish security relationship ended in March 1975 when the Algiers pact between Iran and Iraq closed off Israeli access via Iran to Iraqi Kurdistan. Kurdish autonomy began to emerge, with close US support, following the 1991 Gulf War, and the process accelerated following the 2003 US invasion and occupation of Iraq.

As with the southern Sudanese legacy of appreciation for Israel's earlier support, so in the case of the Iraqi Kurds an important reservoir of goodwill exists, based on the perception that the Jews and the Kurds share a common fate in confronting hostility toward their national aspirations on the part of the surrounding countries.[25] Even Murat Karayilan, the acting leader of the Turkish Kurdish PKK (Kurdistan Workers' Party) guerilla movement, which has been fighting the Turkish government from a base in northern Iraq, has expressed empathy for Israel in view of the two peoples' shared history of "tragedies and genocides."[26] In 2009 a publication called "Israel–Kurd" began appearing in Kurdistan, emphasizing the affinity between the two peoples.[27] Some Israeli scholars have proposed that Israel reach out to the Kurds of northern Syria as well as to those in northern Iraq.[28]

That Israelis and Kurds retain a special affinity that is essentially foreign to the Arabs was demonstrated at a conference in Europe in early 2013, which was attended by more than 100 representatives of the Arab countries and a handful of Kurds, Turks, and Israelis, including the author. At a session convened to discuss Kurdistan in Iraq, all the Kurds attended, as did many of the Israelis and two or three Turks. Not a single Arab chose to participate— as if the Kurdish issue was of no relevance to the Arab world.

When, in mid-2014, the conquest of portions of northern and western Iraq by the Islamist State in Iraq and Syria (ISIS) prompted the Iraqi Kurdish leadership to expand the Iraqi territory under its control and even engage ISIS in armed conflict, Prime Minister Netanyahu responded by publicly recognizing Kurdish "independence." That move was almost certainly not coordinated with the Kurdish leadership and was probably intended essentially as a signal to Washington not to try to rescue Iraq from fragmentation. After all, ISIS's conquest of Iraqi territory could at least temporarily constrain Iran's strategic access to Iraq, Syria, and southern Lebanon, thereby serving Israel's own strategic needs. Nevertheless, the Netanyahu declaration constituted a new milestone in Israeli–Kurdish relations.

## SYRIAN–LEBANESE DISINTEGRATION: NEW LINKS WITH LEVANT MINORITIES?

One of the key characteristics of the Levant is its abundance of ethnic and religious minorities—some, such as the non-Maronite Christian sects, with no territorial base, and others, such as the Alawites, Maronites, Kurds, and Druze, anchored in traditional homelands. If and as Syria and possibly Lebanon disintegrate in the course of the Syrian civil war and the territorial integrity of some of their minority populations is jeopardized by the forces of anarchy and conflict, these territorial minorities may turn to Israel for help, just as their territory could suddenly become relevant to Israel.[29]

There are ample precedents for Israeli–Maronite and Israeli–Druze collaboration. Both groups have a history of contacts with Israel going back to the prestate Jewish Yishuv in Palestine. Syria's disintegration, if it happens, is sure to provoke some Israelis to recall prestate and postindependence

Israeli strategic planning, which at times focused on the ethnic minorities to the north as possible autonomous or sovereign buffers against Arab Muslim hostility (see chapter 5, "The Levant Minorities"). That approach died out after the 1982–1983 fiasco of Israeli–Maronite cooperation, but it could be revived in the event of Syria's collapse.

In particular, a significant interest group has developed among Israeli Druze citizens, who enjoy disproportional representation in the Knesset across the spectrum of Zionist parties and are also represented in the IDF's senior officer corps. As the Syrian civil war ground on during 2013 and 2014,[30] it seemed possible that pressure would be felt in some way to support Syria's Druze if they are threatened by Sunni Salafist revolutionaries.[31] Arab sources described US–Jordanian–Syrian rebel plans for a southern Syria buffer zone, with links to Israel, as well as a possible rebel southern offensive against Damascus. Jordanian sources indicated that joint planning between Jordan and Syria's southern Druze was highly advanced.[32]

At the official level, Israel has also exploited the recent plight of regional minorities to "score points" vis-à-vis the tumultuous Arab and Muslim worlds. Michael Oren, Israeli ambassador to Washington, noted in February 2013 that Israel was the safest haven in the region for the Christian minority. In retaliation for Turkey's expulsion of Israel's ambassador in Ankara following the 2010 Mavi Marmara incident, Foreign Minister Avigdor Lieberman suggested establishing ties with the Kurdistan Workers' Party (PKK), which has fought Turkey for decades.[33]

Still, there are also ample reasons Israel could be deterred from entering into any substantial new contacts. We have noted how Israel's disastrous experience in an alliance with the Maronites in 1982–1983 has soured it on close contact with Middle Eastern minorities ever since. And its experience in 1967 and again in 1982 in occupying Arab territory—followed by two highly problematic unilateral withdrawals (Lebanon in 2000 and Gaza Strip in 2005)—has persuaded it to avoid prolonged occupation in the future at almost any cost. Israel would almost certainly never respond to a Maronite or Druze request for arms or training that was not accompanied by a convincing demonstration that the recipient was capable of defending its own interests actively and independently—a quality distinctly lacking in Levant minorities in recent decades—and that Israeli assistance would not involve occupation of Arab territory.

Of the other territorial minorities, the Alawites and Hezbollah are likely to remain allied with Iran, and the Syrian Kurds are physically distant. But so strong is the perception in the Levant of Israel as a kindred spirit with the region's ethnic minorities that rumors and speculation regarding even Israel and the Alawites abound. In November 2011, advisers to Lebanese Maronite member of parliament Michel Aoun allegedly marketed a new–old Middle Eastern alliance of Jews, Druze, Christians, Alawites, Shi'ites, and Kurds.[34]

And in July 2013, *The Guardian* reported that "[a] mediator—a well-known diplomatic figure—is understood to have been asked by [Bashar] Assad to approach the former Israeli foreign minister, Avigdor Lieberman, late last year [2012] with a request that Israel not stand in the way of attempts to form an Alawite state [on Syria's Mediterranean coast], which could have meant moving some displaced communities into the Golan Heights area."[35]

While neither of these reports appears particularly credible, their relevance lies in the testimony they bear to a "minority solidarity" mode of thinking in the Levant in recent years: a search for an old–new logic in the Levant minority picture. Indeed, because the Levant is truly a mosaic of ancient cultures and religions, layered with the seemingly endless history of conquests by Persians, Greeks, Romans, Byzantines, Arabs, Crusaders, Ottomans, and Europeans, the idealistic notion that it can somehow be made to work as an integrated, multicultural whole has over the years tempted one or another of the minorities, including the Jews of the Yishuv and then Israel.

It was at the Maameltein conference of May 1983, referred to in chapter 5, that we Israelis were treated to an eloquent presentation of the concept by Charles Malik, a Lebanese Orthodox Christian who had served as president of the United Nations General Assembly and was now professor at the American University of Lebanon.

Malik focused on "The Great Land Bridge" of the Levant, between the Taurus Mountains near the Turkish–Syrian–Mediterranean border in the north and Egypt in the south, the desert to the east, and the Mediterranean on the west:

> Jewish revelation, the Christian god and aspects of the Muslim faith were all born here. Most of the time, the region has been ruled by outsiders. Today [1983]—a unique historical juncture—The Great Land Bridge features an unprecedented concentration of intellectual achievement in one part, Israel, while Lebanon's Christians can serve as a vanguard for other Middle Eastern Christians. The Maronites can bridge the chasm between the Vatican and the Jews. Lebanese Orthodox Christians will perform the same function with world Orthodox Christianity. Israel will tell the United States that the Jews' welfare is linked intimately to that of the Maronites. The Great Land Bridge must assert its unique identity: not Middle Eastern, but Mediterranean. One hundred years from now it will number 50 million people and astound the world with its creativity.

Thirty years later, not 100, the Great Land Bridge was in collapse. With the post-Ottoman Levant state system in disarray as a consequence of the revolution and resultant anarchy in Syria, the prospect of beleaguered ethnic and religious minorities to Israel's north reaching out to Jerusalem and seeking support could not be ignored. That is what makes the issue of Israeli ties with Levant minorities far more than an exercise in periphery history.

## CONCLUSION

Note that very senior officials from Azerbaijan, Cyprus, and Greece all visited Israel in the spring of 2013, reflecting a concerted effort by Jerusalem to upgrade its new periphery relations. But is this a viable array of periphery allies? Ephraim Halevy, former head of Mossad and national security adviser, argues that no serious new periphery doctrine is possible without Iran—an ally in the past but now an enemy.[36] A casual glance at the map and at population and economic statistics, to say nothing of assessments of military might, appears to cast doubt on the capacity of Azerbaijan to "balance" or contain Iran or of Greece and Cyprus to contain Turkey, even if Israel's oil deals with Baku and recent eastern Mediterranean natural gas discoveries give Israel's new periphery relationships a stronger economic component than in the original version. Eritrea's international pariah status and consequently its problematic relations with Israel render it less than an ally.[37] And to the extent that Israeli policy planners conceive of the southern European Mediterranean countries as periphery-type allies—one high-level planner actually mentioned Albania and Italy—they appear to be reaching too far both geographically and politically.

Still, these strategic ties undoubtedly benefit all the parties involved. Notably, current Israeli periphery planning is far more systematic and bureaucratized than it was in the 1950s and 1960s. Back then, beyond the original northern and southern triangles concept formulated around Ben Gurion, expansion of the periphery was largely improvised and relied on trial and error. Now the Prime Minister's Office and ministries of foreign affairs and defense are all involved at the conceptual level. Now, too, relations with nearly all the countries of the new periphery are overt, have a strong economic component, and are maintained at the highest diplomatic level—in part a reflection of Israel's enhanced global and regional presence compared to that of the 1950s, at least partially obviating the need for a clandestine approach.

This brings us to the raison d'être for the new periphery. As a contribution toward containing the hostile impulses of Islamists in Iran, Turkey, and possibly Egypt, these axes of containment make sense. Dropping the term "periphery" is also geographically more precise, insofar as Cyprus is closer to Israel than it is to Turkey, which the Israeli–Cypriot–Greek partnership "contains."

Then too, the beginnings of an Israeli rapprochement with Turkey in March 2013 could conceivably at some point affect the Israeli–Cypriot–Greek relationship. Can Israel manage parallel strategic partnerships with both Turkey and the Hellenic countries, two parallel peripheries?

Much of the earlier interactive, strategic dimension is missing in the new periphery. Beyond the Azerbaijani Jewish connection, there is little of the ingathering-of-the-exiles grand strategy of old. And in view of the seemingly reduced US role in the Middle East, there is less interaction with the great power grand strategy, though Israeli officials do judiciously try to market the axes of containment concept to their counterparts in Washington, and Azerbaijan is anxious to recruit Israeli support in the United States.

Nor does the new periphery present anything like the aspiration of a formal alliance of the sort represented in the past by Trident; rather, these are ad hoc coalitions. Indeed, much of the security thinking informing the new relationships focuses on intelligence against terrorism and the strengthening of domestic security apparatuses rather than, say, intelligence against mutually perceived hostile states, such as Syria and Iraq, with which Israel periodically found itself at war in the past. Finally, with the exception of possible Israeli Druze pressure to support the Syrian Druze, there is little room left in Israeli strategic thinking for regional minorities, even if a sentimental link remains with the now-autonomous Kurds and the sovereign southern Sudanese.

A problematic dimension to the new periphery strategy emerges when contemplating the possibility that some official planners might welcome it as reflecting a decision by Israel to turn its back on its Arab/Islamist neighbors and/or to despair of ever resolving the Palestinian issue. This orientation appears to be reinforced in particular by the emerging relationship with European Union members Cyprus and Greece, on the one hand (here and there reflecting wishful thinking as if Israel belongs to Europe!), and the rise among Israel's immediate neighbors of political Islam with its hostility toward Israel's very existence, on the other.

The original periphery was largely confined to the Middle East, focused on a hostile Arab core, and was designed and used at least in part to encourage peace with the Arabs. We have noted in this context that Israel's peace treaty with Egypt has already lasted longer than Trident ever did. The new periphery, in contrast, reaches beyond the Middle East to Central Asia, Europe, and Africa and involves a perceived Islamist core that is still evolving but that perforce includes former periphery friends. Yet this new periphery, too, should ideally be intended not only to contain but also to promote coexistence with Israel's immediate neighbors, however problematic they may be and despite the fact that much of the new periphery does not border on the Arab world.

Israel's new periphery relationships are undoubtedly useful in both security and economic terms. They offer a measure of strategic depth in the Mediterranean, Africa, and Asia. And they send an important message to the Islamists in Iran, Turkey, and Egypt that Israel can muster regional assets and resources toward containing the Islamists' more dangerous inclinations, but not much more than that. Neither Cyprus nor Azerbaijan can muster the strategic critical mass needed to contribute to Israel–Arab peace the way the shah of Iran and King Hassan of Morocco once did. Turkey's looming regional power presence in the Middle East is hardly balanced—if indeed that is necessary—by the friends Israel is cultivating along its borders: "Romania, Bulgaria, Greece aren't worth a thing," a senior Israel Foreign Ministry planner told me, voicing concern lest our periphery interests distract us from pursuing positive avenues, such as the Arab Peace Initiative of 2002.

Then too, there is a side to these new periphery relationships that should be familiar from our investigation of the cynicism that informed the attitudes toward Israel of its original periphery allies in the region. In unvarnished conversations, key Greek and Cypriot figures characterize their attitude toward Israel as pragmatic and possibly temporary. They don't hide their opinion that Israel in its isolation had best treat them fairly and with fewer displays of bravado. Such candid conversations are virtually impossible to arrange in Azerbaijan and Ethiopia, but the sentiments are probably no different. We have already noted the superfluous and potentially damaging nature of Israeli boasts regarding an Azeri threat to Iran.

The Gulf emirates perhaps could help Israel improve relations with its Arab neighbors, but they won't as long as Israel is not more forthcoming regarding the Palestinian issue. Besides, we're no longer dealing with enticing Anwar Sadat of Egypt to make peace; the best we can hope for is to leverage the periphery to help maintain chilly relationships with Egypt and Turkey and perhaps, here and there, to deter Iran.

Yet Turkey and Israel still need one another in the Iranian context, and the Muslim Brothers in Egypt, if and when they are again in power, will need Israel more than ever to intercede with its many friends in the US Congress. The new periphery, then, should be designed at least conceptually not only to contain Israel's problematic neighbors but also to promote reconciliation with them.

## NOTES

1. Large portions of this chapter are based on not-for-attribution interviews conducted in late 2012 in the Prime Minister's Office and the Foreign Ministry. A portion is based on a not-for-attribution briefing by a senior Ministry of Defense official in February 2013. See also Yoel Guzansky and Gallia Lindenstrauss, "Revival of the Periphery Concept in Israeli Foreign Policy?" *INSS Strategic Assessment*, vol. 15, no. 2, July 2012 (Hebrew and English); David Ignatius, "Israel's Arab Spring Problem," *Washington Post*, July 6, 2012.

2. Ephraim Sneh, *Responsibly: Israel in the Post-2000 World*, 1996, Yediot Aharonot, ch. 5, "The New Periphery" (Hebrew).

3. See Alexander Murinson, *Turkey's Entente with Israel and Azerbaijan: State Identity and Security in the Middle East and Caucasus*, Routledge, 2010.

4. Alex Mintz and Shaul Shay, "Herzliya Forum for Formulating Security Concept," policy paper 1, Mar. 2014.

5. "Air force drills in Bulgaria against air defense systems," *Haaretz*, July 2, 2013; "Joint maneuvers with the Romanian Air Force became public due to a tragic IAF helicopter crash there," *Haaretz*, July 26, 2010.

6. See http://www.novinite.com/view_news.php?id=121535.

7. Nahum Barnea, *Yediot Aharonot* holiday supplement, Apr. 14, 2014.

8. Analysis on Cyprus is based in part on interviews held Nov. 19, 2012, in Nicosia with energy journalist Gary Lakes, energy official Solon Kassinis, academic Harry Tsimitas, former MFA official Sotos Zackheos, and particularly attorney Chris Pelaghias.

9. See in this connection, Gabriel Haritos, "Cyprus, Turkey and Israel: Changing Realities and Dilemmas," Tel Aviv University, Dayan Center, *Tel Aviv Notes*, vol. 7, no. 7, Apr. 10, 2013.

10. Communique, Office of the President of Israel, May 7, 2013.

11. Oleg Vukmanovic and Ron Bousso, "Insight: Israeli gas holds promise of better ties with neighbors," *Reuters*, Apr. 14, 2014.

12. For a comprehensive survey of these issues see Simon Henderson, "Natural Gas Export Options for Israel and Cyprus," Mediterranean Paper Series 2013, German Marshall Fund, Sept. 2013.

13. Zvi Magen, "Russia and the Middle East: Policy Challenges," Tel Aviv, INSS Memorandum no. 127, May 2013, p. 60.

14. Interviews conducted in Athens, Apr. 9–10, 2013, with Gerasimos Arsenis, Dr. John Nomikos, Professor Sotiris Roussos, Dr. Andrew Liaropoulos, and others.

15. Sneh interview; see also Jean-Loup Samaan, "Israel Looks Beyond the Region for Strategic Partners," *Al-Monitor*, Oct. 25, 2013; Cnaan Liphshiz, "With eyes on neighbors, Azerbaijan and Israel intensify ties," *JTA*, Sept. 17, 2013.

16. Michael Segall, "Iran Fears Growing Israel–Azerbaijan Cooperation," Jerusalem Center for Public Affairs, Jerusalem issue brief, vol. 13, no. 12, May 17, 2013.

17. *Haaretz*, Jan. 20, 2013.

18. *Haaretz*, Nov. 17, 2011.

19. *Economist*, Feb. 4, 2010.

20. Interview with Egyptian diplomat familiar with Israel, Sept. 25, 2012. See also chapter 14, "Arab Reaction."

21. Barak Ravid, *Haaretz*, July 21, 2013.

22. *Yediot Aharonot*, Feb. 12, 2013.

23. Younes Abouyoub, "Morocco: Reforming the Constitution, Fragmenting Identities," *Arab Reform Bulletin*, Carnegie Endowment for International Peace, July 6, 2011.

24. Dayan Center invitation, Tel Aviv University, May 2014.

25. Uri Lubrani interview. See also Ofra Bengio and Oded Eran, "Israel and the Kurdish Spring," *Haaretz*, Feb. 26, 2013.

26. Jonathan Spyer, "Fire from the Mountain," Gloria Center, Oct. 31, 2010.

27. Eldad Back, "They haven't lost hope," *Yediot Aharonot* Sabbath supplement, Nov. 13, 2009. Back presents numerous additional expressions of friendship encountered in Iraqi Kurdistan.

28. Ofra Bengio, "Israel should reach out to separatist Syrian Kurds," *Al-Monitor*, Jan. 15, 2014; Gallia Lindenstrauss and Oded Eran, "The Kurdish Awakening and Its Ramifications in Israel," *INSS*, vol. 17, no. 1, Apr. 2014 (Hebrew).

29. This analysis is based to a large extent on the author's paper, "As Syria descends into chaos: challenges to Israel," http://peacebuilding.no/Regions/Middle-East-and-North-Africa/Israel-Palestine/Publications/As-Syria-descends-into-chaos-challenges-to-Israel.

30. For a comprehensive survey of the Syrian Druze during the rebellion, correct as of Mar. 2013, see http://www.fpri.org/articles/2013/03/syrian-druze-toward-defiant-neutrality.

31. Jodi Rudoren, *IHT*, May 24, 2013; *Times of Israel*, Mar. 31, 2013; Oraib Al-Rantawi, "Off the Terrorist List," Al-Quds Center for Political Studies, Feb. 27, 2014.

32. "What really happened in Jordan: behind the scenes of the Syrian buffer zone proposal," *Al Bawaba*, Mar. 2, 2014; Phil Sands and Suha Maayeh, "Israel 'buying' information on extremists from rebel groups," *The National* via *Al-Monitor*, Mar. 2, 2014; Ehud Yaari, "The battle for southern Syria heating up" (quoting Arab sources), *Washington Institute Policy Watch* 2253, May 14, 2014; conversation with senior Jordanian official, July 2014.

33. Cited in Clive Jones and Beverley Milton-Edwards, "Missing the 'devils' we knew? Israel and political Islam amid the Arab Awakening," *International Affairs*, vol. 89, no. 2, 2013, pp. 399–415.

34. "Aoun is marketing a 'minoritarian' gathering including Jews," *Al Rai al Aam*, Nov. 14, 2011, reported in "Daily Briefing," Mideastwire.com.

35. *The Guardian*, July 22, 2013.

36. Halevy interview.

37. Sneh interview.

## Chapter Fourteen

# Arab Reaction

In the 1950s, 1960s, and 1970s, Israel sought to leapfrog over its hostile Arab neighbors and link up with non-Arab and non-Muslim countries and minorities on the Middle Eastern periphery. What did those Arab neighbors think about this then, and what do they think about it now?

Any attempt by an Israeli to collate and assess Arab reactions to the periphery doctrine is almost by definition subjective and limited in scope. Still, it is illuminating: whatever we can glean about Arab attitudes will be useful on two levels. First, alongside the objective evidence that relates to the periphery's influence on Israel's involvement in war and peace with its Arab neighbors, knowledge of Arab attitudes can contribute to an assessment of the relative success or failure of the original periphery doctrine. Second, understanding the Arab response can perforce contribute to a better understanding of what might make a new periphery doctrine work in terms of Israel's overall relationship with the region, including its Arab and other Islamist components.

The Arab reactions to the periphery doctrine outlined here can be divided roughly between the general—those presenting a broad Arab view of an Israeli grand strategy—and the specific—pinpoint responses from Egypt, Palestine/Jordan, and Lebanon and Syria.

### GENERAL ARAB ASSESSMENTS

Saad Eddin Ibrahim is a former adviser to Egypt's president Gamal Abdel Nasser. In later life, as a leading Egyptian liberal and human rights campaigner, he was imprisoned for three years by President Hosni Mubarak. He takes—from an Arab standpoint—a relatively lenient attitude toward the periphery doctrine.

> Part of what we grew up [with] as teenagers and later on as young intellectuals is that Israel has grand schemes, . . . has lived in fear of being surrounded by the Arab world. It is strategizing to surround the Arab world with a tier of its own like-minded, if not enemies, but non-Arab allies . . . enemies of our enemies. . . . [I was] trying to alert fellow Arabs . . . how clever the Israelis are, and how it behooves us to be smarter if we want to either overcome or neutralize the Israelis.

Confronting Israel's current effort to establish a kind of new periphery to outflank Arab, Iranian, and Turkish Islamism, Ibrahim acknowledges that this "makes sense to a fearful neighbor." On the other hand, "if [Israel is] seen to be developing a new periphery, this feeds right into [a] search for a scapegoat. . . . You will always have people who will still think that there is an Israeli or a Zionist or a Jewish conspiracy behind everything. . . . We need a new enemy."[1]

Israel as scapegoat, against the backdrop of the periphery doctrine, has been a particularly popular theme in Egypt since the revolutions began in January 2011. In conversations held eighteen months into that revolution, in August 2012, one Egyptian Muslim Brotherhood activist told the author, "Israel has to commit to cease plotting with any ethnic or religious faction to destabilize Arab countries." What ethnic and religious factions was he referring to? He couldn't name any. A moderate secular Egyptian noted that the SCAF, Egypt's temporary military rulers, were planting conspiracy rumors regarding Israel specifically to take the heat off the army.

Abdel Monem Said Aly, like Ibrahim an accomplished Egyptian strategic thinker and former head of the Al-Ahram Center for Political & Strategic Studies, defines Israel's periphery rationale along similar lines:

> In simple words Israeli grand strategy, in addition to other dimensions like the organic link with the USA and the use of the horrible memories of . . . WWII, is for Israel to ally itself with countries surrounding the Arab world plus make a coalition with minorities who for historical reasons detest Arabs and/or have no interest in the Arab Israeli conflict. Hence [Israel] was building [a] special relationship with Turkey, Iran, Ethiopia, South Sudan, Maronites, Kurds and the like.

But Said Aly is far less forgiving than is his fellow Egyptian Ibrahim: "This strategy added to the Egyptian perception of Israel as the wrong state in the wrong place. Encircling the Arab world particularly in the 1950s and 1960s was particularly antagonistic to the idea of Arab nationalism."[2]

Hussein Agha, an Arab closely involved in Palestinian politics for over four decades, offered an illuminating political science–based analysis of what has worked and not worked for Israel regarding the periphery. He distinguishes between circumstances in the past conducive to Israeli links with non-Arab states as opposed to today's emerging Islamism, which favors Israeli links with minorities:

> There's a very long-standing and quite pervasive belief that part of the Zionist scheme . . . is to instigate and facilitate the fragmentation of the Arab world. . . . This is a way in which the Israelis and the Zionists weaken the Arabs. As long as [Arab] nationalism is the order of the day, making an alliance with the periphery states makes sense, but making an alliance with . . . the minorities does not make sense. . . . Nationalism, which is not based on religion . . . is a melting pot. . . . Syria takes all the constituents of Syria and becomes a Syrian nation; Lebanon, the same. . . . As long as nationalism is the order of the day, the minorities, it's very perilous the kind of relation you can have with them, and they have not succeeded. [Even] the Kurds . . . did not ally themselves openly with you in a relationship where you benefited from them in a clear way. . . .

> [When] Islam takes over, then Muslims stop being potential allies. . . . Turkey and Iran will stop being allies. . . . On the contrary, they become a source of threat. [Whereas] minorities . . . become potential allies. . . . And now you have a potential with the Maronites, . . . with the Alawites, with the Kurds it can be much more meaningful, with the Druze, with all kinds of minorities who would feel, in this wider sea of Sunni Islam, more vulnerable, while under nationalism. . . . the ideologues of nationalism came . . . from minorities.

And yet, looking at the new periphery and in contradiction to his admonition about Muslims not being potential allies for Israel, Agha points to Azerbaijan and the other "stans": "Iran is very, very worried about Azerbaijan."[3]

Ahmad Khalidi, a Palestinian intellectual based in London and Oxford, who has also closely advised the PLO leadership, focuses on Trident and Egypt: "Nasser's main strategic thrust was to confront what he perceived as being the alliance between Turkey, Iran, and Israel," a pact he thought the West was creating. Nasser ignored the weaknesses of Trident—the lack of a serious intelligence or operational payoff—and saw it as a threat.[4]

## EGYPT

It is with regard to the flow of Nile waters from the heart of Africa to Egypt that Arab, and specifically Egyptian, preoccupation with the periphery doctrine reaches a genuine degree of paranoia. Egypt's existential focus on the Nile is understandable: it is the exclusive source of water for nearly all of Egypt's burgeoning population (at the time of writing, over eighty-five million). In recent years, Cairo has found itself at odds with many of the Nile-source riparian states regarding upstream exploitation of Nile waters and the great lakes from which they flow. Uganda, Ethiopia, Kenya, Tanzania,

Rwanda, Burundi, and the Democratic Republic of Congo have all signed an agreement to seek more water from the Nile before it flows to Sudan and Egypt. They have their own development needs and refuse to recognize the validity of a 1929 colonial treaty guaranteeing Egypt the lion's share. Since 2011, with revolutionary chaos seemingly weakening Egypt, the Africans have been emboldened and encouraged to challenge Cairo's claims.

Ethiopia, the source of 80 percent of the Nile waters reaching Egypt via the Blue Nile, is moving ahead toward construction of the Grand Ethiopian Renaissance Dam, Africa's biggest hydroelectric project. Addis Ababa assures Egypt and Sudan that they will actually benefit from the dam, which is being constructed by an Italian firm with financial assistance from China. Sudan appears satisfied with Ethiopia's explanations, but not a few observers and experts in Egypt intimate that the dam will deny Egypt water and could even lead to war between Egypt and Ethiopia.[5]

Note that Israel's relations with most of the Nile riparian states, now including South Sudan, go back many decades. Beyond all these undisputed facts, it must be added that there is not an iota of evidence that Israel has ever plotted to divert Nile waters bound for Egypt or that it is doing so in the era of the new periphery. Yet none of this prevents Egyptian and other Arab media from accusing Israel of plotting ceaselessly to do so. The fact that Israel provides water expertise to some of the Nile riparian states is cited as evidence and so are occasional visits to African countries by outspoken Israeli officials, such as Foreign Minister Avigdor Lieberman, who is known for threatening in the past to attack Egypt's Aswan High Dam.

Here is a brief representative selection of accusations regarding alleged Israeli plots to divert Nile waters, taken from the Arab press in recent years:

- London-based *Al-Quds Al-Arabi*: "Israeli infiltration in Africa is targeting Egypt and the future of its people by hitting it where it hurts, i.e., the water of its Nile."
- The United Arab Emirate's *Al-Khaleej*: "[I]mplementation of the Israeli project for controlling the water of the Nile has entered an advanced phase . . . under . . . American blessing."
- *Al-Jazeera*, quoting Egypt's minister of Irrigation and Water Resources Mohamed Bahaa Eddin: "We totally reject any sort of Israeli presence in any Nile Basin country."
- Egypt's *Al-Masryoon*: "Egypt informed Israel that it rejected its funding of dams in Ethiopia and Tanzania."
- The United Arab Emirate's *Al-Bayan*: "Israel's role in inciting the upstream states against Cairo amounts to blackmail."
- Egypt's *Al-Youm Al-Saba'a*, quoting deposed President Hosni Mubarak: "Africa is full of Jews; they played a role in the plan to build a dam at the sources of the Nile."[6]

Perhaps of greater concern to Israel are remarks made by generally level-headed and analytical Egyptians who know Israel well, such as Abdel Monem Said Aly:

> [O]f most [importance] to Egypt was the increasing influence of Israel south of Egypt threatening the water flow to Egypt. There is not much doubt in [the] Egypt mind that Israel has a great deal to do with the secession of Sudan to two parts, encouraging Ethiopia to build dams on the Nile, and playing with the Nile [basin] states to sign an agreement that [denies] Egypt historical rights. . . . Israel's periphery strategy is adding to the nuclear issue and the Palestinian question [and] makes Israel a national security threat to Egypt.[7]

Omar Suleiman, under President Hosni Mubarak a key Egyptian interlocutor with Israel on security issues, told a very senior Israeli security official in recent years that Egypt was "alarmed" at Israel's presence in Ethiopia because of the Blue Nile issue.[8] Finally, Ahmed al-Muslimani, appointed in July 2013 spokesman for Egypt's interim president, published a book in 2013 that is highly critical of Israel and argues that Ethiopia's dam project is being implemented as part of a Mossad plot to destroy Egypt.[9]

We have already underlined the total absence of any evidence that Israel has ever entertained invoking a water strategy against Egypt or that it in any way supports such a strategy today. That a broad spectrum of Egyptian commentators would persuade us that the southern periphery never died and that it is particularly hostile toward Egypt is little more than a paranoid fabrication. Moreover, today a strong foundation of good relations between Israel and core countries, such as Egypt (and Turkey), remains in place. In cultivating its relations with African countries south of Egypt, Israel should be aware that it is liable to be seen by Egypt, without an iota of objective justification, as fomenting hostile designs against it on a strategic issue of existential importance. But by the same token, because of Egypt's unfounded concerns that focus on it, Israel can potentially, with skillful diplomacy, leverage its African periphery presence into influence in Cairo, whether regarding regional, water-related, or bilateral issues.

## PALESTINE/JORDAN

Generally, since Israel's creation in 1948 the Palestinians have been so preoccupied with their own conflict with Israel that their leaders and intellectuals have devoted little energy to Israel's relations with the periphery. This perhaps renders all the more interesting the theory presented by Marwan Muasher, former foreign minister of Jordan and ambassador to Israel and the United States:

Turkey, Iran, Ethiopia, South Sudan are the countries that have historically had a big problem with the Arab world. And so Israel making friends with [them] was seen as another example of Israel's lack of seriousness in reaching an agreement with the Palestinians. I mean, the Arab world always looked at Israel as finding any excuse to circumvent coming to terms with the Palestinian issue. . . . [B]y creating the impression that you're accepted in the neighborhood because there are countries with which you are friends in the neighborhood was seen by the Arab world as a delusion that Israel puts itself into, that . . . it doesn't have to solve the Palestinian issue for it to be accepted in the neighborhood.[10]

If Israel has over the decades linked up with the periphery ostensibly to escape dealing with the Palestinian issue, it is only in the Palestinian context that this survey encountered an attitude of mockery toward part of the periphery itself. Thus an intriguing comment on Israel's periphery ties in the Palestinian connection was made by Faisal Husseini, a prominent West Bank–based leader of Fateh and the PLO, shortly before his death in May 2001. Professor Shlomo Avineri of the Hebrew University addressed Husseini at a conference in Jerusalem: "I can't understand you. I have no problem accepting the Palestinian right to self-determination, why do you have problems granting the same right to the Kurds?" Husseini replied, "The Kurds are not a nation or a people, just a bunch of mountain tribes."[11]

Implicit here is an Arab rejection of nationhood or people-hood status for non-Arab peoples in the Middle East, including the Jews of Israel. The Kurds are tribes, the Jews mere coreligionists. This is reminiscent of a famous comment by Egyptian diplomat Tahsin Bashir in the 1980s. Referring to all Arab countries other than Egypt, with its 7,000 years of history, Bashir called them disdainfully "tribes with flags."

## LEBANON AND SYRIA

We have already noted, in chapter 7, the interest displayed by first the Yishuv and then the state of Israel in the Levant minorities, particularly the Maronites and the Druze. The fact of that interest has never been lost on the minorities themselves or on the Sunni Arabs, in whose midst they live in Lebanon and Syria. Joseph Bahout, a Maronite intellectual well connected in both French and Lebanese political circles, relates that he was brought up in Beirut to view Israel as interested in strong links with non-Sunni minorities to weaken classic Arab nationalism. This, in his understanding, is the Levant view: Israel is conspiring to support minorities to fragment Arab states. A second Lebanese strategic analyst, a Sunni who preferred to remain anonymous, seconded this perception.

In this regard, Bahout notes that Shimon Peres's "Greater Middle East" project, launched at the height of the Madrid- and Oslo-inspired peace process in 1993–1995, was welcomed by the Sunni Arab mainstream in Syria and Lebanon precisely because it was seen as a "soft power" reversal of the periphery doctrine: here was Israel asking to integrate with the mainstream and not with the minorities. The latter, according to Bahout, opposed Peres's idea precisely for this reason. Bahout adds that at present, in a Middle East increasingly Islamized, the Maronites are themselves reaching out to other regional minorities: they are, for example, the main investors in the Kurdish tourist sector in northern Iraq.[12]

Peres's Greater Middle East project, incidentally, died due to both lack of progress toward a two-state solution and lack of enthusiasm on the part of Arab economic actors for Israeli entrepreneurship and investment in infrastructure projects. Israel, the Arabs were suggesting, could integrate in the Arab Middle East only if it solved the Palestinian issue and accepted a weak, passive status as a minoritarian state.

Two Syrian Sunnis, one a prominent academic and both involved in the revolution against the Assad regime, hence both preferring to remain anonymous, also subscribed in conversations in 2012–2013 to the view that Israel favors Levant minorities against the Arab mainstream. Despite the absence of any evidence of serious Israeli–Alawite ties, one related a popular belief among Syrian Sunnis that Israel helped Hafez Assad seize power in Damascus after the 1967 war in return for his "giving" Israel the Golan—a concession no self-respecting Sunni Arab nationalist would make. The other pointedly asked the author, "If Assad falls, will Israel help the Alawites?"[13]

## CONCLUSION

Undoubtedly, anecdotal evidence regarding Arab reaction to the periphery doctrine cannot form the basis for anything but a speculative and incidental contribution to our attempt to describe and understand the periphery doctrine at work. After all, the outflanking doctrine that is described here by Arabs as an expression of Israeli hostility was in fact, in Israeli eyes, a reaction to Arab hostility.

Certainly, we can conclude that the periphery doctrine, much of which was handled as a clandestine operation, was known to the Arabs more or less in real time and that it was understood as an attempt to weaken Arab power. And we can also assert, on the basis of the evidence mustered here, that Arab understanding of Israel's motives was varied and uneven.

Today, in contrast, Israel makes little attempt to hide its modest new periphery aspirations. This begs the question: Is it advisable for Israel to seek constructive ways to explain its new–old doctrine to regional Islamists, precisely to allay exaggerated Islamist assessments of Israel's capacity to fragment and undermine and to instill a more constructive approach on their part toward Israel and its motives? Or is Israel best advised to allow the exaggerations and fears to take root, to better leverage what influence it can muster from the periphery on the Islamist attitude toward it? Conceivably, too, Israel can learn something from these Arab comments that is applicable to today's more limited periphery thinking: Israel will be scapegoated by hostile Arabs regardless of its periphery contacts, and fellow non-Arab and non-Muslim minorities in the Middle East will be drawn to Israel in response to Islamism.

## NOTES

1. Interview with Saad Eddin Ibrahim, Europe, Sept. 2, 2012.
2. E-mail correspondence with Abdel Monem Said Aly, Sept. 3–4, 2012.
3. Hussein Agha interview, Europe, Aug. 31, 2012.
4. Ahmad Khalidi interview, Europe, Aug. 31, 2012.
5. For a short review of the Nile water situation, see Katrina Manson, *Financial Times*, June 30, 2012.
6. See, respectively, *Al-Quds Al-Arabi* (London), Sept. 4, 2009; *Al-Khaleej* (UAE), Apr. 27, 2012; *Al-Jazeera* website, Aug. 2012; *Al-Masryoon* (Egypt), May 7, 2010; *Al-Bayan* (UAE), Apr. 26, 2010; quoted in *Yediot Aharonot*, Sept. 24, 2013.
7. Said Aly e-mail correspondence.
8. Shabtai Shavit interview, Israel, Dec. 25, 2011.
9. Haggai Erlich, "The Struggle over the Nile: Ethiopians and Ethiopia," Dayan Center, *Tel Aviv Notes*, vol. 7, special edition no. 2, July 17, 2013.
10. Marwan Muasher interview, Europe, Sept. 1, 2012.
11. E-mail correspondence with Shlomo Avineri, Oct. 29, 2009.
12. Interview with Joseph Bahout and second Lebanese, Europe, Feb. 15–16, 2013.
13. Conversations in Europe, Sept. 1, 2012, and Feb. 16, 2013.

*III*

# Conclusion

*Chapter Fifteen*

# Can Israel Find a Regional Identity?

Did the periphery doctrine provide Israel in its early decades with a regional identity? Can a new periphery approach do that today? Is a regional identity a vital attribute of Israel's overall strategic well-being, and if so are there alternatives to a periphery doctrine? These are the questions that this concluding chapter seeks to answer.

## PERIPHERY TIES AS ALLIANCE

Meir Amit, who as head of the Mossad from 1963 to 1968 was intimately involved in developing the periphery doctrine, defined it in 1999 as "part of a world view, strategic thinking that is designed to create a true alliance with all the actors in the Middle East who are not Muslim Arabs." And he added, "This issue constantly energized us to establish links with a large number of countries and actors in the region who are not integrated into its classic [Arab Muslim] fabric."[1] Allowing for the fact that we have expanded Amit's definition to include peripheral Arab countries—Yemen, Oman, Sudan, and Morocco, and here and there commercial ties with the Gulf emirates—his framing of the doctrine offers a solid basis for assessing its achievements and failures and their strategic ramifications for Israel.

Undoubtedly, the periphery doctrine reflected a "world view" and "strategic thinking." We have argued that it constitutes a clearly thought out grand strategy, one of several generated by David Ben Gurion and his close advisers in the early years of the state. In some ways it had roots in the prestate minority doctrine developed by the Jewish Agency's Political Department under Moshe Sharett and others. Overall, and notwithstanding failures and limitations, Ben Gurion emerges from a study of the periphery doctrine—particularly when the doctrine is viewed as part of a cluster of parallel grand strategies that included an opaque nuclear capability, a great power alliance, and mass immigration—as a strategic genius.

Did the periphery strategy involve "all the actors of the Middle East who are not Muslim Arabs," as Amit suggests? Never, though not for lack of trying or at least interest on Israel's part. Repeated initiatives to link up in some form of alliance with the Druze of the Levant never reached fruition. And the Egyptian Coptic Christians, the Christians and Druze of Syria, and the Amazigh of the Maghreb never entered into significant relations with Israel, though strategic ties with Morocco during the time of General Oufkir could be construed to constitute a kind of indirect periphery relationship with a branch of the Amazigh. Certainly, at the conceptual level the periphery doctrine was directed at "all the actors" specified by Amit.

Yet the periphery doctrine most emphatically never generated a "true alliance," even if many Israeli protagonists of periphery ties used that term. This is a crucial concluding determination. Typically, in international relations an alliance is understood to constitute a close and formal association of nations or other groups that is formed to advance common interests or causes. Even if—bearing in mind the difficulty Israel would have experienced in demanding written agreements from, say, the shah of Iran or Mullah Mustafa Barzani—we ignore the stipulation of formality, it is difficult to characterize any of Israel's periphery relationships, past and emerging at present, as a true alliance.

Rather, in the past, these were by and large relationships of convenience on the part of Iran, Turkey, Morocco, and Ethiopia. From the standpoint of Israel's state partners, ties were based on shared antipathy toward and fear of militant Arab nationalism. Israel was understood to be a desirable partner due to its military and intelligence capabilities and its close links with Washington, attributes that were at times embellished with seemingly anti-Semitic exaggerations about Jewish international reach, which Israel's operatives generally chose to ignore or even cultivate. Because the assets Israel brought to the alliance table were limited, the partnership could be downgraded or severed by the other side, and this indeed happened whenever it suited Israel's partners in view of their calculations regarding the Arab world.

Some Israeli practitioners and operatives chose to view the relationships as embracing the kind of moral commitment and emotional and historical link we see, say, in the NATO alliance or the US–British relationship. As a new player on the Middle East scene, yet an ancient people carrying a very heavy burden of persecution, isolation, and genocide, Israel has—at times desperately—sought acceptance and ratification as a legitimate regional actor. This undoubtedly injected an emotional element into Israel's own perception of its periphery relationships, just as it did with the early peace treaties with Egypt and Jordan and the internationally sponsored multilateral baskets of the early 1990s. But this idealistic approach—"realizing a dream"—has never been seriously reciprocated at a significant state level, whether periphery or core.

Only in the Kurdish and southern Sudanese links could a genuine sense of fellowship or brotherhood of Middle East minorities be said to have prevailed and even to have weathered serious mutual disappointment on each side regarding the performance of the other in crucial areas. Some of the Israeli proponents of the brief alliance with the Lebanese Maronites entertained illusions of a genuine commonality of interests; few of the Maronites did, and the ultimate disappointment and disillusion were so strong that Israel has avoided similar minority entanglements ever since.

Nevertheless, and bearing in mind that at a certain level all international relations are based on self-interest, Israel's aid to fellow regional minorities, which faced at times brutal Arab hostility, was an impressive chapter in Israel's history as a modern nation-state. Even when, in the case of the Maronites, Israel's empathy was misplaced, it was nonetheless genuine. For a country that itself has been under prolonged siege and attack by Arab neighbors, this is a record that Israelis and friends of Israel can take pride in.

Turning to the new periphery, or axes of containment, it seems clear that Israel's developing relationships with countries bordering or close to Turkey, Iran, and Egypt cannot be termed formal alliances, however beneficial they are to both sides. One obvious reason is that Israel has no reason to perceive itself in such an adversarial relationship with Turkey and Egypt as to justify alliances against them. It maintains relations with both and had in the course of 2013–2014 adequate justification for courting improved relations with them although, interestingly, the July 2014 Israel–Hamas war brought Egypt closer to Israel while alienating Turkey. Another is that all the "containment" candidates continue to maintain ties with Turkey, Iran, and Egypt—relations that could improve or deteriorate in accordance with fluid international developments. Note in this context that Greece and Turkey continue to be members of NATO, which is indeed a formal alliance. And Azerbaijan was being courted by Iran in mid-2013 as Tehran, under a new president, sought to improve relations and even mediate the Azeri–Armenian Nagorno-Karabakh dispute.[2]

Accordingly, it would be a mistake for Israeli strategic planners to perceive new periphery relationships as reflecting a zero-sum reality vis-à-vis Israel's Islamist neighbors. The new periphery offers Israel substantive economic benefits (natural gas, oil, arms sales) and limited military benefits. It can be exploited for these advantages by both sides—Israel and its periphery partners—but the nature of the perceived Islamist threat, which the new periphery is conceived to counter or contain, is so fluid and the backdrop of peace agreements and contacts with Arab and Islamist regimes still residually viable enough that it would be foolish for Israel not to seek to remain a genuinely regional player.

As we shall see, such a flexible approach can even conceivably offer Israel regional strategic benefits that exploit its contacts with both periphery and core. In some ways, had there not been an earlier periphery doctrine from the 1950s, 1960s, and 1970s to use as a term of reference and a model, Israel's contemporary core–periphery concept could equally well be understood as simply a mosaic-like dynamic of friends and enemies—neither fully defined—in the greater Middle Eastern region.

## A COST–BENEFIT ASSESSMENT

The inevitable conclusion of a cost–benefit assessment of the periphery doctrine as it played out in the years between 1956 and 1983 is that on balance, it was a success: the benefits clearly outweighed the costs.

What were the benefits? The periphery links, with states and minorities alike, including specific periphery-oriented operations, such as the 1960s effort in Yemen, the Entebbe operation, and the *aliyah* of Ethiopian Jewry, contributed to an image of Israeli power, regional reach, and deterrence. Of particular note is Trident, which brought Israel into a relationship with the two largest and most influential non-Arab states in the Middle East, and the Ethiopia and southern Sudan relationships, which projected, in Egyptian eyes, a threat to the Nile waters. In Ephraim Halevy's words, "[W]e became a regional player . . . as well as an international player."[3] And by casting Israel as a regional player, the periphery doctrine also obliged its Arab neighbors to deal with it as a Middle East polity rather than—as their propaganda portrayed her—as a European colonialist implant.

Thanks to this image and to the efforts in 1976–1977 of the shah of Iran and King Hassan of Morocco, the periphery doctrine contributed to peace with Egypt. The contention that the periphery delayed or sabotaged peace does not appear to be supported by hard evidence—beyond the temporary negative effect on relations with Egypt of the 1982 invasion of Lebanon and the Iran–Contra affair. (Needless to say, other Israeli acts not connected or indirectly linked to the periphery also damaged relations, for example, the 1981 destruction of Iraq's Osirak reactor within days after an important Israeli–Egyptian summit meeting and prolonged neglect of commitments regarding the Palestinian issue.) There is no specific evidence to support the contention that prior to 1977 governments of Israel rejected feelers regarding peace or even nonbelligerency with Egypt because of periphery considerations. (Again, peace feelers were rejected, but for other reasons.)

Nor could periphery alliances ever replace peace with the Arabs or alleviate the need for it. Here we have already noted that despite a host of obstacles and even revolution, the Israeli–Egyptian peace has already lasted longer than Trident did and that even if seen as little more than a nonbelligerency pact, its strategic benefit for Israel exceeds that of Trident manyfold.

Periphery ties were extremely useful to Israel in developing two additional grand strategies. They bolstered the strategic and intelligence relationship with great powers—Britain, France, and particularly the United States—and they facilitated the mass immigration of Jews from Morocco, Ethiopia, and Iran.

The periphery doctrine also was generally inexpensive to maintain. The Kurdish and southern Sudanese operations each cost less to maintain than did a single contemporary fighter aircraft. A number of the relationships—Trident, Ethiopia, Morocco—facilitated arms sales along with development of civilian economic ties and cheap Israeli energy imports. The arms drops to Yemen—as usual, surplus arms and booty from wars—were extremely cost effective in terms of damage to Egypt's military capabilities at what proved to be a critical time: the eve of the Six-Day War.

Only one periphery operation ended up being extremely costly in terms of financial outlay, Israeli international prestige, and particularly, Israeli lives: the 1982–1983 First Lebanon War, which was based on the Maronite connection and Ariel Sharon's design to force the Palestine Liberation Organization to move from Lebanon to Jordan, where it would "Palestinize" the Hashemite Kingdom. But that fiasco was not the only area where Israel paid a price for the periphery. Another was Iran–Contra, the ultimate expression of the problematic phenomenon of periphery nostalgia, wherein Israeli relations with the United States and Egypt were negatively affected.

Then there are what can only be termed "costs" of omission. Despite Israel's hopes and expectations, its periphery "allies" generally did not lift a finger to support it militarily during the 1967 and 1973 wars (though here and there they offered useful wartime intelligence). This is where critics of the doctrine find the greatest fault. Israel was, and still is, a country struggling for survival in a hostile environment, and periphery links were intended at least in part to alleviate this dilemma. Instead, wartime situations produced periphery indifference (Trident), symbolic aid and comfort to the enemy (Morocco in 1973; Iran and the oil embargo in 1973; Iranian assurances to Iraq in 1973, which allowed the latter to send a large portion of its forces to the Syrian front), outright refusal to deploy units as previously agreed to alleviate military pressure on Israel (the Kurds), and avoidance of passing on certain knowledge of the 1973 surprise attack (Morocco and possibly Iran and the Kurds). In this last context, the only explicit warning Israel received in 1973 was from an Arab neighbor, Jordan's King Hussein.[4]

These drawbacks are linked to another: the fragile and unpredictable nature of periphery ties and even of US support for them, which were at times considered vital. Thus the shah and apparently the United States as well could pressure Kurdish leader Barzani not to help Israel in 1973. The shah could toy with seriously downgrading the relationship with Israel in 1975 because he sensed—tragically and mistakenly, as it would turn out—that he could get a better deal from the Arabs, Uganda's Idi Amin could cut Israeli access to southern Sudan in 1973, and Prime Minister Begin could fail in 1977 to persuade US President Carter to back a revived relationship with Ethiopia. Put differently, Israel was generally unable to sustain its periphery relationships on a completely independent basis, thereby rendering them that much more shaky and unreliable.

On the other hand, it is arguable that Israel's periphery connections in any case never really aggrandized its political stock in Washington, which was and is dependent on nonperiphery-related issues and actors. Moreover, as Ephraim Halevy notes, also there was and still is a danger of overreliance on Washington:

> We in practice nearly destroyed our regional capabilities because we rely on Washington. At the end of the day we have Congress, we have the White House, we have the media, we have AIPAC [American Israel Public Affairs Committee]. That's not only Netanyahu's concept, it was Sharon's. I'll sit with Bush, we'll wrap up the matter, then we'll call the others and tell them "these are the terms of the agreement." I think this was a colossal mistake. Not that we'll crown kings in the periphery, [but] we use our connections in the periphery.[5]

The potential pitfalls of an Israeli–US periphery connection are liable to be amplified at a time when in any case the United States is reducing its regional profile and withdrawing from active involvement in many parts of the Middle East.

## LESSONS FOR A POSSIBLE NEW PERIPHERY

Israel currently confronts the growing influence or threat of political Islam in neighboring countries (Egypt, Gaza, southern Lebanon, and Syria) as well as more distant ones (Turkey and Iran). Iranian use of the Red Sea, in coordination with Sudan, to transfer weaponry to anti-Israel Salafis in Sinai and Gaza, constitutes an additional Islamist threat. Accordingly the delineation of a new periphery, variously defined as axes or circles of containment, or arcs, is a legitimate policy objective for the strategic planning establishment in the Prime Minister's Office, the Defense Ministry, and the Foreign Ministry. We have described these axes as comprising a set of countries surrounding Turkey—Cyprus, Greece, Bulgaria; Azerbaijan to the north of Iran; and Ethiopia, South Sudan, Kenya, and possibly Eritrea on Israel's southern flank where they embrace the Nile Basin and Israel's southern maritime approaches. And we have noted that unlike in the case of the original periphery, the nature of the current Islamist core calls into question the very rationale of dividing the Middle East into core and periphery.

What lessons can we derive from our examination of the classic or original periphery that will facilitate a better understanding of the benefits and pitfalls of a new periphery approach?

Beginning with the western and northern spheres, flanking Turkey and Iran, the candidates for this new periphery are nowhere near the strategic caliber of the old. Trident partners Iran and Turkey were regional powers, capable of intimidating their Arab neighbors; this gave Israel an enhanced deterrent profile. In contrast, Cyprus and Greece are in serious financial straits and militarily weak, Bulgaria is corrupt and backward, and Azerbaijan is a tightly run dictatorship ruling over a small population base. Israeli strategic planners may fantasize that a foothold in the eastern flank of the European Union renders Israel somehow a Mediterranean or even European power, and they may bluster that the link with Azerbaijan causes the powers that be in Tehran to tremble over potential subversion via Iran's large Azeri minority. But this posturing is unconvincing. The western and northern spheres do comprise very important energy elements—the natural gas partnership with Cyprus and possibly Greece and oil deals with Azerbaijan.

The new–old southern sphere is more impressive insofar as it counters radical Arab and Islamic influence and balances Egypt's sway in the region.

To the extent that Israel's outreach to a new periphery emanates from a sense of despair regarding prospects for coexistence with an Islamizing Middle East, it is also unconvincing. The current Islamist ring of hostility is nowhere near as daunting as was Nasserist Arab nationalism in the 1950s, 1960s, and 1970s. During the first half of 2013 alone, we witnessed the beginnings of Israeli rapprochement with Turkey, the reassertion of secular power and influence in Egypt, and according to sources quoted in Tel Aviv and Amman by interviewer Jeffrey Goldberg, closer Israeli–Jordanian relations in anticipation of threats from anarchic Syria, Salafi terrorism, and the "Shi'ite arc."[6] By mid-2014, with Israel at war with Islamist Hamas in the Gaza Strip, it was possible for Major General Amos Gilad, director of political–military relations at the defense ministry, to claim that Israeli "security cooperation with Egypt and the Gulf states is unique. . . . The Gulf and Jordan are happy that we belong to an unofficial alliance. . . . [Saudi Arabia] has signaled a relationship in recent weeks."[7] Nor did Israeli dialogue with the Muslim Brotherhood in its diverse regional manifestations appear to be a total impossibility, particularly if progress toward a two-state solution with the Palestinians could be demonstrated. Seen in this context, any new periphery must not be allowed to become part of a zero-sum core–periphery game that renders it impossible even to attempt dialogue with the Arab world and Islam.

Rather, precisely because of the relative weakness of the new periphery and the relative openness of the new core compared to the old, Israeli strategic planners should look for ways to exploit both new and old regional ties to Israel's advantage by bridging core–periphery conflicts through creative diplomacy. For example, Israel has excellent relations with Ethiopia and South Sudan and ongoing security cooperation with Egypt. The latter is understandably extremely concerned that construction of the Grand Ethiopian Renaissance Dam on the Blue Nile in Ethiopia will reduce its vital water supply—an issue over which some Egyptians even level baseless accusations against Israel. Meanwhile, in South Sudan the Jonglei Canal project to bypass the swampy Sudd region and enhance the flow of the White Nile for Egypt's benefit is still on hold after two decades of conflict. Not only must Israel take extreme care to allay occasional Egyptian concerns lest it connive with Ethiopia and others on sensitive water issues, but it could conceivably use its access to the southern periphery in this context, particularly if it can recruit US or other third-party backing, as a means of leveraging better relations with Egypt through the offer of water recycling technology, discrete mediation, and good offices.

On another periphery front, Israel would ideally wish to be in a position to sell its Mediterranean natural gas to Turkey—the most efficient way to export this resource—yet without compromising its developing cooperation with Cyprus and possibly Greece. Here, even if Israeli–Turkish relations warm up, the Turkish–Cypriot conflict over north Cyprus seemingly prohibits the close regional cooperation necessary to exploit Cyprus' and Israel's gas resources in coordination with Turkey. In contrast, by mid-2014 Egypt's energy crisis was so acute that Cairo was openly discussing the purchase of Israel's Mediterranean gas. Here again is an area where creative diplomacy on Israel's part could conceivably bridge the current perception of a core–periphery gap.

Of course it is possible, perhaps even probable, that Israeli attempts to bridge perceived core–periphery gaps between Egypt and Ethiopia and Turkey and Cyprus will fail because one or both sides reject it as an interlocutor. In that case, at least Israel will have taken a step to fortify its credentials as a regional player and an unbiased neighbor. In view of a variety of regional and international efforts to isolate Israel, this can hardly hurt its global status and sense of self-respect.

In concluding this section on applying lessons from the old periphery to the new, two additional issues command our attention. One is intelligence: our discussion of the fall of the shah, the collapse of Trident, the abortive Iran–Contra affair, and periphery nostalgia revealed a clear lacuna regarding Israeli intelligence on Iran. Either those in charge of assessment regarding Iran were denied important operational intelligence, or their assessments were ignored.

Precisely because Israeli minister of defense Ezer Weizman knew the shah personally, he apparently saw no need to ask his own intelligence establishment if 1978 was the right time for Israel to sell Iran sensitive weapons technology. And when only a select few Israelis knew that Professor Moshe Mani was treating the shah for leukemia, they did not bother to share this secret of far-reaching ramifications for the entire Middle East with those charged with assessing the shah's chances for survival.

At issue is the inclination of high-level Israelis in dealing with an autocratic and highly centralized yet friendly regime, to avoid defining it as the object of intelligence collection and to rationalize their monopoly of sensitive information on the basis of both secrecy and their certainty that they know the regime in question better than anyone else. This syndrome is not relevant to friendly countries in the new periphery, such as Cyprus, that are democratic and offer bountiful sources of overt information and easy access to an open society, but it is highly relevant to the more autocratic regimes of the new periphery where early warning of change is vital.

A second issue of possible relevance for the new periphery draws on Israel's links with downtrodden minorities, such as the Kurds and the southern Sudanese in the old periphery. We have noted several instances in which, based on the statements of senior Israeli operatives and officials, a strong moral and humanitarian element became one of the motives for Israeli involvement. This approach apparently drew upon both homegrown values developed in Israel as it overcame regional isolation and, as Yitzhak Rabin testified in the case of the Kurds, Jewish values. Taken together, these are an important source of stability and inner strength for Israel to draw on. There is some evidence that they inform or influence Israel's current friendship with the newly independent state of South Sudan.

Looking to the future in this regard, the collapse of the post-Ottoman Levant state system in Syria and possibly in Iraq and Lebanon as well is liable to place Levant non-Arab and non-Muslim ethnic groups in serious jeopardy. In examining the prospects and contingencies surrounding a possible new periphery of minorities, Israel should not abandon these very positive values that motivated its actions in the past, even if in terms of realpolitik they are negligible. At the same time, it must take care not to allow its sincere intentions to be exploited cynically, as the Maronites did in 1982, and it should take care lest involvement with a neighboring minority generate domestic discord within Israel.

## IRAN AND PERIPHERY NOSTALGIA

Our remarks about the danger of making decisions regarding autocratic states in the new periphery without a foundation of adequate, independent intelligence also apply to contemporary Iran. As noted in chapter 10, there are significant decision makers in the Israeli system who appear to have convinced themselves that Israeli action against Iran can bring down what they perceive to be an artificial and rootless regime and restore to power the "real" Iranians, Israel's friends. This advocacy of regime change appears to reflect lessons not learned: a dangerous lack of understanding regarding the nature of Israel's original periphery alliances and the regimes they relied on as well as the inclination of a people who perceive themselves to be under attack, in this case the Iranians, to rally round the regime, whatever its nature. Periphery nostalgia as even a minor consideration with regard to an attack on Iran could conceivably have dangerous consequences.

## ALTERNATIVE STRATEGIC DIRECTIONS

A periphery approach, past and present, is a response to the perception that Israel is regionally isolated. In an era of Arab revolution and ascending political Islam, this is an understandable perception. One Washington-based Middle East expert, Robert Satloff of the Washington Institute, observed in June 2012 that "viewed from Washington or Jerusalem, the upheavals of the last 18 months [i.e., since the beginning of the Arab revolutions] have transformed an already difficult regional landscape into perhaps the most inhospitable strategic environment in modern history."[8] A year later a prominent Israeli columnist, Nahum Barnea, observed after yet another coup in Egypt that "[e]vents like this drive many Israelis to isolationism. They see on TV the frenzied mob . . . the tanks and armored vehicles in city streets, the generals whose uniforms sag under the weight of medals celebrating victories that never happened, the religious fanaticism alongside the nationalist fanaticism, they watch and say: what links us to them? Like that old saying of Ehud Barak, we're a villa, they're a jungle."[9] Another appropriate metaphor might be the new high-tech start-up that was suggested tongue in cheek by an Israeli humorist, whereby an innovation backed by President Shimon Peres would simply detach Israel from the Asian mainland and float it westward to Europe.[10]

This is the atmosphere that produces the kind of periphery outreach strategy that would be defined as a zero-sum game. Yet as we have already seen in looking at ways to leverage the periphery in the interests of coexistence with the core, this is a dangerous approach. Barnea himself goes on to caution Israelis that "[w]hether we like it or not, our fate is interwoven" with that of the Egyptians. "Egypt is a stabilizing factor in the region, a moderating factor. Israel has a direct interest in its success."[11] Israel's new periphery partners appear to understand this, too: with increasingly Islamist Turkey in mind, Greece and Cyprus were the first European Union member states to welcome the advent to power of the anti-Islamist General al-Sissi in Egypt in mid-2013.

With unprecedentedly strong US backing and in view of the near total absence of a conventional military threat by its neighbors in the foreseeable future, Israel confronts a variety of ways to counter strategic isolation by projecting power, both hard and soft, in several directions.

Israeli arms sales and military cooperation extend far beyond the new periphery to India, China, and Europe. A British document leaked in 2013 points to Israeli arms sales (comprising British components, hence requiring British government approval) in 2011 to Egypt, Algeria, the United Arab Emirates, Morocco, and Pakistan, with the British refusing to license re-export by Israel to Russia, Sri Lanka, India, Turkmenistan, and Azerbaijan.[12] There is undoubtedly an even longer list of global clients for Israeli arms that do not comprise British parts. Plans for natural gas sales focus on Jordan and the Palestinian Authority, Egypt, and Turkey as well as more distant markets in the Far East and Europe. Another area of both hard and soft power projec-tion is countries in the region that quietly look to Israel for both deterrence and a broad range of technology exports. There is apparently even room for strategic coordination with Saudi Arabia, based on a shared regional threat perception.

Much closer to home, at the very core, Jordan, the West Bank, and even Egypt are potential consumers of Israeli desalinated water or desalination technology—a field in which Israel leads the region. All in all, the eastern Mediterranean Sea offers Israel a new dimension of strategic depth in terms of both barely exploited resources and security—the latter reportedly an-chored in second strike–capable submarines.

Israel's overall economic potential, particularly in the energy, high-tech, and military fields, appears thus far to be relatively immune to the kind of economic boycott that Israel's international critics are increasingly advocat-ing. Taken together, these dimensions of power-projection potential give Israel an enhanced degree of strategic maneuverability. In this spirit, one conservative Israeli think tank head, Ephraim Inbar, argues that "[a] closer look at Israel's interaction with countries near and far . . . belies the claim that it is isolated. In fact, Israel is increasingly acknowledged as a world player in view of its social, economic, technological, financial and diplomat-ic achievements."[13]

So is Israel as isolated as a villa in a dangerous jungle? Or is it a success-ful global player? In a way, both descriptions fit. Yet what is striking about both questions is that they perforce ignore the issue closest to home, the one generating the impression of growing isolation: the Palestinians. While in the near future the Palestinian issue is not liable to precipitate a major Arab–Israel war, the demographic existential threat it projects to Israel's very being as a Jewish, Zionist, and democratic state only grows with every new

Israeli settlement, every neighborhood encircling Arab East Jerusalem, and every new expression of Palestinians' frustration with the prospects of a state of their own—even if the Palestinian camp bears a significant portion of the blame for this state of affairs. Soothing reassurances from the prosettler camp to the effect that this problem will somehow solve itself are, to put it mildly, lacking in strategic objectivity—indeed, lacking in strategic essence, insofar as they are messianic. It is in this Palestinian context that the European Union poses the only likely and conceivably viable economic boycott threat to Israel.

This narrative is not about the Palestinian issue. By and large, the periphery strategy operates on a different plane—one of many areas of Israeli strategic endeavor that reach far beyond the Palestinians. Yet, in contemplating discussion of some sort of new periphery—axes of containment—and its contingencies and alternatives, the Palestinian issue cannot be ignored.

If Israel cannot separate itself from the Palestinians in a two- or three-state solution (the latter conceivably comprising the Gaza Strip as a distinct political entity), it risks drifting into de facto apartheid or some form of binational Jewish–Arab state. A two- or three-state solution leaves Israel ideally suited to pursue both a new periphery strategy and accommodation, to the extent possible, with Arab and even Islamist neighbors—in other words, to integrate into the mosaic of Middle East countries. In contrast, even if a new periphery is projected to blossom far beyond this author's expectations and indeed contain Israel's Islamist neighbors, the apartheid-like state increasingly contemplated by Israel's dominant and complacent prosettler right wing would be a repugnant partner internationally.

Only Israel's weak new Mediterranean area periphery partners—Hellenic Orthodox Christian states that have problems of their own with Islamist neighbors and face mass illegal Muslim immigration—might not be overly troubled by a negative Israeli image. But as we saw in looking at the Cypriot and Greek response to Israel's strategic outreach, even they are aware of Israel's regional isolation and are wary of its requests and requirements in the military sphere.

And if, eventually, after failing to separate itself from the Palestinians in the West Bank and Gaza, Israel folds into a binational state where the Jews are destined to become a minority, it won't need a periphery doctrine or any other grand strategy. It will simply fit all too nicely into the Muslim Arab Middle East core.

Thus, alongside a determined attempt to expand relations with a new periphery, anti-Islamist Arab neighbors, and the new Islamist core—and alongside global reach and the exercise of hard and soft power—Israel must come to grips with the Palestinian issue in a far more realistic way than hitherto. Otherwise, all its grand strategies will be jeopardized. Indeed, one could argue that all the grand strategies generated by Ben Gurion nearly sixty years ago now require a serious reassessment in view of global and regional events and the direction Israel's own strategic development has followed.

During the early decades of its existence, Israel displayed considerable ingenuity, originality, and adaptability in developing grand strategies for dealing with almost overwhelming existential threats and nation-building challenges. The original periphery doctrine, with its mix of wisdom, compassion, sense of purpose, and even a pinch of cynicism, played a central role in this integrated and broadly successful effort. Today's challenges require the display of similar capabilities on Israel's part. Its current performance falls disappointingly short of Ben Gurion's standard.

## NOTES

1. Meir Amit, Introduction to Eliezer (Geizi) Tsafrir, *Ana Kurdi*, 1999, Hed Arzi (Hebrew).

2. See Timur Saitov and Gallia Lindenstrauss, "The extended conflict over Nagorno-Karabakh: Can Iran succeed where the Minsk group failed?" *Zman Iran*, no. 38, July 10, 2013, ACIS, Tel Aviv University, http://humanities.tau.ac.il/iranian/he/pre/9-iran-pulse-he/241-zman-iran-38-july2013.

3. Ephraim Halevy interview.

4. Pesach Malubani, *Mabat Malam* 67, Nov. 2013 (Hebrew).

5. Ephraim Halevy interview.

6. Jeffrey Goldberg, Interview with King Abdullah II, *The Atlantic*, March 18, 2013.

7. Quoted by James M. Dorsey, "Israel and Saudi Arabia: Forging Ties on Quicksand," RSIS Commentaries, July 7, 2014.

8. Robert Satloff, "America, Israel, and the strategic implications of the Arab uprisings," *Times of Israel*, June 2, 2012.

9. Nahum Barnea, "Thunder from Cairo," *Yediot Aharonot* weekend supplement, July 5, 2013.

10. Thomas L. Friedman, "Bits, bytes and bombs," *IHT*, Mar. 25, 2013, quoting Ari Shavit, who is quoting Amnon Dankner.

11. Barnea, July 5, 2013.

12. Alistair Dawber, "Pakistan denies receiving weapons and security equipment from Israel," *The Independent*, June 22, 2013.

13. Efraim Inbar, "Israel is not isolated," *BESA Mideast Security and Policy Studies*, no. 99, 2013.

# Heads of Mossad

Reuven Shiloah, 1949–1952
Isser Harel, 1952–1963
Meir Amit, 1963–1968
Zvi Zamir, 1968–1974
Yitzhak Hofi, 1974–1982
Nahum Admoni, 1982–1989
Shabtai Shavit, 1989–1996
Danny Yatom, 1996–1998
Ephraim Halevy, 1998–2002
Meir Dagan, 2002–2011
Tamir Pardo, 2011–

# Persons Interviewed

## ISRAEL

Nahum Admoni, former head of Mossad
Uzi Arad, former senior Mossad official, former national security adviser
Shimon Avivi, former senior Mossad official
Avner Azulai, former senior Mossad official
Zvi Bar'el, Israeli journalist
David Ben Uziel, former senior Mossad official
Shlomo Gazit, former head of IDF Intelligence
Ephraim Halevy, former head of Mossad, former national security adviser
Shalom Harari, former senior IDF officer, Islamic affairs expert
Alouph Hareven, former senior Mossad and MFA official
David Kimche (deceased), former senior Mossad official, former MFA director-general
Uri Lubrani, former ambassador in Tehran and Kampala, senior Defense Ministry official
Bruce Maddy-Weitzman, Tel Aviv University
Shlomo Nakdimon, Israeli journalist
Menahem Navot, former senior Mossad official
Amir Oren, Israeli journalist
Yitzhak Oron (deceased), former senior Mossad and MFA official
Shimon Shamir, Tel Aviv University
Shabtai Shavit, former head of Mossad
Efraim Sneh, former deputy minister of defense
Dov Tamari, former commander of Sayeret Matkal
Officials in Israeli Prime Minister's Office, MFA, and Ministry of Defense (names withheld at their request)

## ARAB WORLD

Hussein Agha, senior associate, Saint Antony's College, Oxford
Joseph Bahout, Lebanese–French scholar
Egyptian diplomat familiar with Israel (name withheld at his request)
Saad Eddin Ibrahim, sociologist and human rights activist, Cairo
Ahmad Khalidi, senior associate, Saint Antony's College, Oxford
Marwan Muasher, former deputy prime minister and foreign minister of Jordan, former Jordanian ambassador in Israel and the United States
Abdel Monem Said Aly, former head of Al-Ahram Center for Strategic Studies, Cairo
Retired senior Lebanese military officer (name withheld at his request)
Syrian Sunni academic (name withheld at his request)
Syrian Sunni opposition activist (name withheld at his request)

## UNITED STATES

Daniel Kurtzer, former US ambassador to Israel and Egypt
Sam Lewis (deceased), former US ambassador to Israel
Trita Parsi, president, National Iranian American Council
William Quandt, former National Security Council Middle East adviser
Bruce Riedel, former senior CIA official, former National Security Council Middle East adviser
Former senior US diplomat in Middle East (name withheld at his request)

## CYPRUS

Maria Hadjipavlou, University of Cyprus
Solon Kassinis, director, Energy Service, Ministry of Commerce, Industry and Tourism
Gary Lakes, energy journalist
Chris Pelaghias, European Rim Policy and Investment Council
Harry Tsimitras, director, PRIO Cyprus Centre
Sotos Zakheos, retired diplomat

## GREECE

Gerasimos Arsenis, former minister of defense
Andrew Liaropoulos, University of Piraeus
Ioannis Nomikos, George Protopapas, and Thalia Tzanetti, Research Institute for European and American Studies
Sotiris Roussos, University of Peloponnese

# Map 1

## *The Original Periphery Concept*

**1.** The original periphery concept

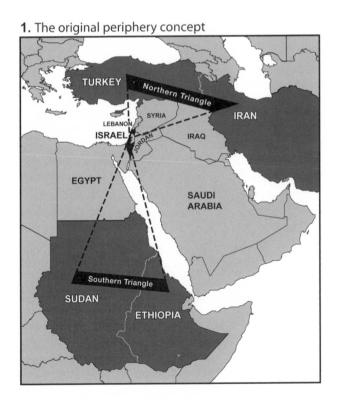

# Map 2

*The Expanded Southern Periphery*

**2.** The expanded southern periphery

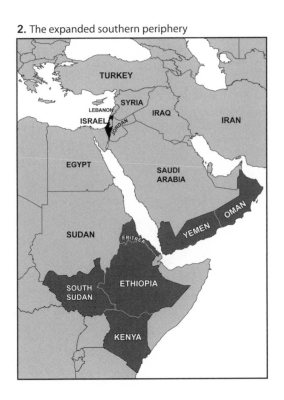

# Map 3

*The Ethnic Periphery*

**3.** The ethnic periphery

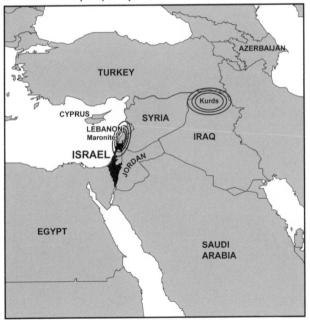

# Map 4

*A New Periphery?*

**4.** A new periphery?

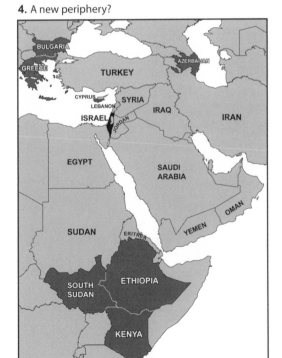

# Index

# About the Author

**Yossi Alpher** served in Israeli military intelligence and the Mossad. Until 1995 he was director of the Jaffee Center for Strategic Studies at Tel Aviv University, where he also edited its publications. In July 2000 he served as special adviser to the prime minister of Israel during the Camp David talks. In 2001 he published *And the Wolf Shall Dwell with the Wolf: The Settlers and the Palestinians* (Hebrew). From 2001 to 2012 he was coeditor of the *bitterlemons.net* family of Internet publications. Alpher lives in Ramat Ha-Sharon near Tel Aviv, where he comments frequently on Israel-related strategic affairs. *Periphery* draws extensively on his intelligence career.